THUMBON●MICS™

THUMBONOMICS™

The Essential Business Roadmap for Social Media & Mobile Marketing

Heather Lutze

Books may be purchased for sales promotion, etc. in bulk by contacting the publisher at:
Findability Press
5750 DTC Parkway, #170
Greenwood Village, CO 80111
303-841-3111

Screenshots have been used with permission of © Facebook, Inc., © Google, Inc., © LinkedIn Corp., © Twitter, Inc. and © WordPress, Inc.

Cover Design and Cartoons: Josh Alves, JoshAlves.com
Book Shepherd: Judith Briles
Editing: Leslie Miller and John Maling (EditingByJohn)
Book Design and Layout: WESType Publishing Services, Inc.

Library of Congress Catalog Number: 2011939448

ISBN: 978-09838667-0-1

1. Social Media   2. Marketing   3. Business   4. Search Engines

First Edition: Printed in the United States

Dedication

Thumbonomics is dedicated, first and foremost, to my wonderful and so patient husband Mark. He has been my rock and my counselor for the past 17 years! You were there for my first book all the way. Once again, I would not have been able to get this one done without him. Thank you, my love. Evan and Kyle—I also could have never finished this book without your love and understanding.

Next, I want to thank my staff at Findability Group who helped me edit, add content and find the tools that were most relevant and helpful for each chapter. They tolerated my endless work on the book and the interviews. Finally, their complete dedication has always ensured that we deliver a service product with integrity and purpose—I will always be so grateful for their hard work.

I also want to say thank you to Steve Lishansky. Without his undying belief in my abilities and encouraging me to ask for what I am worth, I would not have the strength to write this book. Thank you for believing in me and helping me to grow my business to a whole new level. You are amazing!

Contents

Introduction

Inspiration often shows up in the most unlikely of places, just like the idea for *Thumbonomics* did at Denver International Airport.

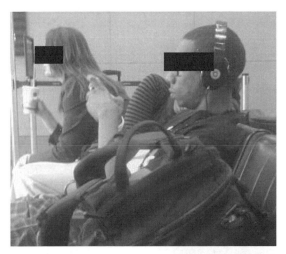

I realized in that moment, that as a business owner, your company may be obsolete if you don't move to the community of "thumb" users fast. This is how people communicate and how they stay connected. They buy here, talk here, search here and live here. This is where your market is growing and thriving—you MUST engage in *Thumbonomics* now!

Thumbonomics is not standing in judgment of how prospects and buyers want to engage with your product or service, it's about being everywhere they NEED to find you quickly and easily by whatever device they choose, i.e. tablet, smartphone or computer. It's your job as executives and marketers to just be there when they search for you. "Adapt or Die!" is our new motto! Let's get to work.

Turning a Blind Eye

I understand why you are ignoring social media.

You think Facebook and Twitter and You Tube and LinkedIn are for younger generations. You think social media is a passing fad. You think it's dumb. You don't want it in the workplace. The word "tweet" to describe Twitter messages sets your teeth on edge ... and who the heck cares what anyone had for lunch? The very name of *social* media is proof positive that it doesn't have a place in the business world—it's for *social* purposes.

And most of all, it's not your demographic.

I get it. I hear you.

The thing is, I heard these exact same comments 10 years ago when I was talking to clients about having a website or setting up email. *The exact same comments!* My clients insisted that their customers weren't on the web, their customers didn't use email. What was wrong with calling instead of emailing? Why not mail out a brochure instead of having a web site?

You get the picture.

And so do I. About your resistance, I mean. For example, I don't care about snowboarding. I'm over 40 and I'm sticking with skiing. I'm willing to innovate a little; I've switched to shape-skis and crooked poles, but I'm not learning snow-boarding. It's for the younger generation.

Plus, at the time it came out and maybe I could have learned it, I was sure it was just a trend, and skiing would prevail. How wrong was I about this? Snowboarding is here to stay. Created in 1963, it got the public's attention—the sport grew exponentially when fiberglass boards were introduced in 1979. Now a mega-million dollar business, it continues to grow by leaps and bounds every year. Lucky for me, there are no negative consequences from my resistance to snowboarding. No penalty to me for being wrong about it or missing the opportunity to learn it a few years ago. It wasn't a fad, it was a trend.

That is *not* the case with you continuing to turn a blind eye to social media.

The Time Is NOW

This is the most fascinating and innovative time in marketing in the the history of marketing. Get excited about this inexpensive and dynamic medium that can change your company and how it markets to its ideal customer.

You have got to get on this bandwagon ... and the sooner the better. I'm going to make it painless for you (that's the whole point of *Thumbonomics*) but you've got to do it. And you've got to do it NOW.

How well did waiting to have a website serve you? Did you miss out on all the best URLs because you waited? Does someone else actually own the URL with your name on it? Did your competition beat you because they were there first?

Ask yourself this question seriously: *How well did your resistance to the web, to email or to voice mail serve you?*

I hear you groaning. You probably feel like you just got the whole web thing down—search engines and SEO and Pay Per Click (PPC) and your new blog—or maybe you're not even there yet. And now you're seriously being asked to take on social media?

This may, at first read, seem very negative and not you at all. I promise, hang in there, and I will take you to the next level. If you have been putting social media marketing off, then we will give you the business foundation and ROI to understand why you should do this full throttle. Still wondering if you should include social media in your marketing plan this year?

In a word: *yes.*

Why? The numbers speak for themselves.

Social Media Stats Are Staggering

Social media is not your demographic? *Are you sure? Pew Internet* and the American Life Project along with *ComScore* in March of 2010 revealed:

- YouTube is searched on more than Yahoo! On a daily basis, there are **3.7 *billion searches on YouTube.*** Yahoo! has 2.8 billion.

- *One in three adult American Internet users* has set up a social media site.
- The average age on Twitter is 31. On LinkedIn it's 41. For Facebook, it's 33. Not your demographic????????
- In 2011, there were *647 million* searches on Facebook each month. That means Facebook's presence as a major search engine is solid ... and Google is watching it like a hawk.

Can you hear me now?

A lot of the pushback I get about social media comes from key executive leadership teams who don't feel like their audience is there. Look at these numbers. Chew on them. The audience *IS* there.

Social Media Sites Have Become Search Engines

It's not only that your customers and prospects are on these sites; they're also *using them for search*.

If you want to be "findable" on the Internet, you can't ignore the fastest growing search engines on the planet; yes, Social Media sites are search engines. My dear friend Annie gave up Facebook for Lent! Why would she do that? Because she recognized that she was addicted to Facebook. It had become her portal to the world and her sole source for information, communication and searching for all the things she needed for day-to-day life.

Go to *Facebook.com* and see what's happening there. Look in the upper right hand corner of Facebook. See the box that says "Search" at the top of my Facebook page:

People are now leaving these portals up all day long, and they're constantly sourcing them for information. They're looking to solve the pain factors in their lives and their businesses, not by looking at your website alone, but by seeing what other searchers are saying ... and what they're saying about you and your brand.

Sorry to say, your website is no longer enough. Even if you've added a blog, or an interactive element, your website is not enough to optimize your "Findability." Things have changed. Search is more of a *conversation* now, not just a one-way street.

> Social media sites are a key element of your company being found and ranked in search engines on the web.

Let's Get Excited and Act Now!

Many companies have been hit hard by the recession, and you, as a result, have been forced into seeing your business in a whole new light. Referral sources you once were accustomed to, have vaporized, and you are now looking forward. I want to encourage you in the fact that you are already on the right path by purchasing *Thumbonomics* and seeing the potential of your company's continued growth on social media sites.

The great part of social media marketing is that it's FREE. With the right tools and effort, you can get Findability via the mobile tools like smartphones, iPhones, iPads, tablets and the trusty desktop or laptop computer and access a new, more qualified customer base than ever before.

Thumbonomics is about being present and accounted for when the searchers needs your help on their terms, NOT yours. You show up to help them; you are their hero because you were there in Twitter, Facebook, LinkedIn, Blogging and YouTube when they needed you the most. You did not stand in judgment of how they wanted to find you, you were everywhere and you were found!

Thumbonomics will teach you how. I've given you a brief overview: now it's time to drill down in detail … Chapter 1, *The Social Media Revolution*, awaits you.

Before You Get Started ...

QR Codes Make *Thumbonomics* Interactive

As I started to write *Thumbonomics*, I wanted to make sure that it could stand the test of time. After all, few areas of technology are moving faster than social media, smart phones and mobile marketing. I was conflicted about writing a book on social media marketing in the first place because many of the tools and sites mentioned might quickly become obsolete.

Then it occurred to me that I could use QR codes to help the book stay current. I had already written the chapter about QR codes—what better way to show off their use! I have incorporated one of these *"Digital Thumbprints"* at the end of each chapter to connect you digitally to the tools presented in the chapter. The QR codes serve several purposes:

- I want to encourage you to give me feedback.
- Let me know about any amazing marketing tools out there that I haven't heard about.
- Extend the life of the book over time, keeping the suggested marketing tools for each chapter current.

- Send me your review of the book.
- Give you ideas for ways your business can take advantage of QR codes.

What Is a QR Code?

 A QR code (abbreviated from Quick Response code) is a specific *matrix barcode* (or two-dimensional code) that is *readable* by dedicated QR *readers, smartphones,* and, to a less common extent, *computers with webcams*. The code consists of black modules arranged in a square pattern on a white background.

You can find them in magazine ads, business cards, on any kind of product, even stitched into fabric. To scan them requires a smartphone with a camera and a "reader app." When the user scans the code, it will display text, contact information, promotional offers, or a web page.

Who Is Using QR Codes?

QR codes are on the upswing in popularity, with no slow-down in sight. A 2011 report released by *ComScore* showed 14 million U.S. mobile phone users scanned a QR code in June alone. Of those people:

- Approximately 61 percent were male;
- More than 50 percent were between 18 and 34 years of age;
- More than a third had a household income *greater than $100,000;*

- Users are most likely to scan codes found in newspapers, magazines and product packaging; and
- They usually scan codes while at home or in a store.

Sound like a market you'd like to tap into?

The 14 million people who used QR codes in June 2011, represent only 6.2 percent of the total U.S. mobile audience. However, smartphones are here to stay, so QR codes will become increasingly popular—*as savvy marketers like you* start coming up with more ways to use them.

According to *Ad Age*, QR codes are a real game changer for marketers. They can make virtually any product interactive; they are readily customizable and best of all—QR codes *are easily trackable*. As a marketer, you can view the amount of times any code was scanned, by whom and even with what kind of device.

How to Use the QR Codes in This Book

Scan the QR code (using a Droid or iPhone) at the end of each chapter and you will be taken to a unique *chapter tools and comments* page. I look forward to hearing from you!

Download an Application from iTunes or your Droid marketplace. Search for the QuickMark application as it works for both types of phones.

Once you have finished reading a chapter,

Please follow these steps:

1. Pick up your smartphone and go to the Mobile App Store. Droids go to the marketplace and iPhones to the App Store.
2. Search for "QR" in the App Store or marketplace. Download the first free app on the list. It will appear on the app screen when the download is finished.
3. Open the brand new app.
4. Scan QR code with application by holding over QR code and waiting until it reads the code.
5. Click "open" to watch video or open link in the browser.

At the end of the first chapter, you will be introduced to the first QR code of 16 that will wrap up each chapter. Scan it with your phone to watch a video on how to use QR codes throughout *Thumbonomics*.

Have *fun* and email us at *Support@Findability.com* with any questions, or call 303-841-3111.

1

The Social Media Revolution

It's All about the Customer and NOT about Your Company!

Are you on Twitter, Facebook, YouTube, LinkedIn, and are you blogging? Like it or not, your website and your company image is being talked about right now on Social Media. *Thumbonomics* is about being EVERYWHERE your customer is, despite what your company thinks is right or wrong marketing mediums for your business. Your job as a marketer for your company is to be EVERYWHERE they want to FIND you. You cannot stand in judgment of how you want to be found, it's about that searcher's preferences. Just like a thumbprint, each person is an individual and wants different things. It's our job to be there when they need us, not push ourselves on them at every turn.

Why do you think TiVo and DVRs are so popular? A typical customer's attitude is:

> I want what I want, when I want it. No one is the
> boss of me!
> I want to skip, skip, skip and go back to my show,
> and I don't want to be marketed or sold all
> the time.

This is what your potential customer has become accustomed to. Smartphones and iPhones have become the craze because they can customize their own apps, and create custom backgrounds, put fancy rhinestone covers on it and call it "baby." It's a slice of "me"—a perfect expression of personal taste and style.

Why do you think satellite radio is so popular? Jupiter-Research, a division of JupiterMedia Corporation, forecast that the U.S. digital satellite radio market would grow from an installed base of 12 million units in 2005 to 55 million units in 2010, **a compound annual growth rate of 35** percent. People do not want commercials; they want un-interrupted music or programming, when they want it. Satellite radio gives you that freedom to choose and control your environment.

No More "Billboard" Thinking!

The days of the *Billboard off the highway* style of marketing is slowly dying. What are we betting on when we advertise on a major highway? The answer is as old as marketing it-self; we are betting that a percentage of drivers who see the billboard will want what we sell and they will remember it long enough to take action. Prospects now want to customize their experience just like they customize their coffee order at Starbucks.

Grande Latte, Skinny, Sugar-Free Hazelnut Syrup with two Splenda. This is my coffee order. What do you know about me already? I am watching my weight, love sweet things but am not a super hard-core coffee drinker because I did not order a Venti or a Trenta (the largest size). Don't you dare give me a cup of COFFEE! I self-identify, along with millions of other Starbucks coffee drinkers, with my coffee order. Starbucks is happy to oblige. My coffee order is a personalized slice of me! Are you giving your prospect their custom coffee order or are you giving them plain coffee? I want every prospect to be a steaming hot, qualified lead for you. They are happy to get information from you, "like" your company, "follow" your company and eventually buy from your company. Is your company thinking old school or new age?

Here's to 40 years of drinks with your name all over them.

Thumbonomics will bring your company out of your old-style marketing coma and upgrade your company marketing plan to an innovative, customer-focused approach.

Why Your Website Is No Longer Enough

What does your website look like on a smartphone or iPad? Have you checked?

Simply put, websites are no longer the leading edge in marketing on the Internet. No matter how great your website is—even if you've added sound, videos and a flash banner—they're still a fairly static medium based on one-sided communication. What do I mean by one-sided communication? It's when your website is *just you* telling site visitors about your company, products and services—you are talking to them, but are they listening?

Think with me for a moment. Think about most of the websites you have seen. No matter how innovative or earth-shattering a website may be, they're still pretty much all the same: Home Page, About Us, Services, Testimonials, Contact Us.

And, if you break those categories down, what that website is really saying is:

Home page—the main page of *our* amazing website.

About us—in case you wanted to spend all day getting to know our team, location, mission statement, favorite colors, etc.—we have a whole section of our site dedicated *to us.*

Services—These are the things *we do.*

Testimonials—In case you wanted more proof, here are a bunch of other people who we convinced to say nice things, *about us*, on our site.

Contact us—Obviously you want more information on how to contact our amazing team—so here are the ways *we prefer* to be communicated with. As a side note, include address, phone number and a general email contact—give the customer multiple choices, including filling out a form and submitting a question.

And no matter how great the content is, it's mostly a variation on the same old themes: what we offer, why we're different, exceeding expectations, outstanding customer service, really care about our clients ... blah, blah, blah ... we, we, we!

Certainly, your website is an innovation over a print brochure, but even though it's virtual, it's still a brochure. It's not a conversation; it's not an interaction; it's a *marketing* piece. It is a one-sided communication—you are talking about yourself to your consumers, and hope they are listening.

Consumers, web searches and site visitors demand that you give them more than just stagnant, non-changing, brochure-style content. They've seen that for the past 10 to 15 years. They're no longer impressed. In fact, they're bored and skeptical.

The Revolution

Internet users view websites as static entities—even if the sites are updated regularly. Today searchers want more.

They want real-time, current information. They want to be connected with the pulse of what's happening *now*, what people are saying, and what's the latest buzz. They want to feel plugged into the *conversation* on any given product, service, industry or topic.

Users have also become less trusting of websites over time. They don't want to know what you're saying about your own company, they want to know what others are thinking and saying. They want "social proof" that they should work with you. They want to be able to ask other people,

Have you worked with this company?
Do you trust them?
What's their customer service like?
What's their return policy?
Are their products or services any good?

Websites don't provide that.

Social media does. In Real Time ... FAST!

It's not just *people* who want more these days.

So does Google. And what Google wants, Google gets.

Google is looking for current information and social proof about your business as well. Google wants to be on the cutting edge of delivering relevant content; that's their stock-in-trade. So suddenly we're seeing live tweet feeds showing up on the first page of Google search results. Ever since Google bought YouTube, videos are now ranked in the search results.

Little gets by Google. They know that websites are notoriously stagnant, and now they're paying attention to the dynamic, collective conversation about your company. More importantly, Matt Cutts, head of Google's webspam team, publicly announced in December 2010 that Google uses your authority in social networks as a factor in your website ranking. That ranking is revealed on YouTube at:

youtube.com/watch?v=ofhwPC-5Ub4

Actively participating in social media means engaging in a conversation about your company in a meaningful way—with customers, prospects and anyone who wants more information about who you are.

> Social media is a marketing tool that plugs people into your company in a very different way. That's why your website is no longer enough!

Even if you're the most traditional of companies with the most traditional of target audiences, you've got to get your company active in social media. Old school traditional marketing tactics are dead and it's time to innovate ... or watch your competitors slowly gain market share.

Keeping Up

In his 2001 essay, author and futurist Raymond Kurzweil wrote in *The Law of Accelerating Returns*:

> An analysis of the history of technology shows that technological change is exponential, contrary to the common-sense "intuitive linear" view. So we won't experience 100 years of progress in the 21st Century—it will be more like 20,000 years of progress (at today's rate).

Technology changes at such a rapid pace that experts like Patrick Cox, co-editor of *Technology Profits Confidential*, says:

> There has been more technological improvement in the last 50 years than in the previous 5,000. It's a lot to keep up with. Nearly impossible. And so frustrating. As soon as you master the newest thing, it changes.

Nevertheless, you must keep up. By the time *Thumbonomics* goes to print, technology will be changing and evolving once again.

Guaranteed, social media will change too, including the addition of new players and new companies on the scene. My fourteen-year-old, Evan, told me recently that once we "adults" have figured out where the "teens" are, they have long moved on to somewhere else.

It already has. Now it's off the desktop or laptop and on everyone's cell phones.

But social media itself is here to stay and you have *got* to get on this bandwagon.

Maybe you have a great website and you're thinking to yourself that your site really is enough.

I promise you that it isn't.

Users have become desensitized to websites; they're no longer impressed.

Companies with their fingers on the pulse of commerce are using social media in addition to their websites to have a presence and define themselves on the Internet. And they're adding social media components to their websites. They're including twitter streams (lists of live "Tweet posts") of all the tweets that are happening inside a particular company. Social media icons are being integrated as part of the look and feel on the site. They should be posted on every page of your website.

Without these elements, visitors find your site stagnant, boring, stale—and they move on to a competitor that has a more updated, responsive site. What if one of your pages moves or excites the visitor? Giving users the ability to share this page provides an opportunity for your content to spread beyond just your site. This has now transformed your site from a one-way communication tool to a two-way viral marketing site.

Trust

Consumers don't trust websites in the way they used to; now they see them as just another marketing tool. Even testimonials aren't seen as compelling.

I've asked audiences all over the country, "What's the first thing you think of when you read a written testimonial?" And they pretty much all respond the same way: "How do we know the company didn't write that testimonial themselves, or have someone's mother write it?"

Many companies are replacing written testimonials on their websites with video clips because they speak to potential customers in ways that are more *personal, immediate, conversational*; and they make a *real connection.* They feel *authentic* to audiences.

Those words are very important for understanding the power of social media: *personal, immediate, connected, authentic, and conversational.*

Each represent the **#1 Reason** why you need to employ social media to market your company. Consumers are demanding immediacy, authenticity and "proof."

Social media is how you give that to them.

Reason #2 for employing social media is to market your business: *Social Media sites have become the new search engines.*

If you've spent the last few years figuring out how to get your company found and ranked by Google, Yahoo! and Bing, you are in for a surprise. Take a look at these astonishing statistics reported in ComScore in 2010:

- YouTube is searched on more than Yahoo! On a daily basis, there are **3.7 billion searches on YouTube** versus 2.8 billion on Yahoo!
- **Facebook is the #8 search engine in the world, and rising.** In the upper right hand corner of each Facebook page—the prime real estate—is a box that says "search."
- Twitter statistics are growing. The Pew Research Center reports that 13 percent of Americans online use Twitter.
- Eighteen percent of online American Hispanics use Twitter. Twitter grew 27 percent in the third quarter of 2010 alone.

Plus, the June 3, 2011, TLNT revealed in its article, *Some Social Media Stats That Even Surprised Us*, that:

- Adults who are 74 and older quadrupled their social networking presence since 2008—making them the fastest growing demographic.
- Older users saw a huge increase in the use of social media. In May of 2010, 43 percent of the 55-64 population were users.
- The percentage of all adult Internet users who watch video online jumped to 66 percent in May of 2010, up from 52 percent two years prior.

We said some of this in the Introduction to get your attention, and we're repeating it here to drive home this point:

If you want to be found when people are searching for your product or service on the Internet, you must employ social media.

What's the Difference Between Social Media and Search Engines?

Google is a search engine for information. You get rankings based on:

- history and longevity
- the richness and relevance of the content
- how often the site is refreshed
- the number and value of inbound links
- and many other factors.

A site earns its ranking over time.

Social media is a different kind of search engine. It's more of an immediate search vehicle, providing up-to-the-minute information and high relevance to whatever specific area is being searched or researched. It's a *real-time* search engine based on this hour, this day, this week. History isn't a factor.

This is such an important fact that even the traditional search engines are taking notice and know they must plug into social media as well.

Google—the #1 search engine—understands that websites are mostly static, non-changing entities and that the market is moving beyond them, i.e., Facebook. Today, *updates from Facebook profiles and tweets from Twitter are starting to show up in search engine results.* Don't let the significance of this escape you.

Google is aware that consumers want more real-time responses to a search. They haven't let the social media trend get past them. Make sure you don't either. *Findability* **is the End Game.**

The endgame for using social media in your organization is to improve your SEO (search engine optimization): in other words, to increase your Findability in the search engines.

In the case of my own company, I would never have started down the social media path if it were still about what someone had for lunch or what their new puppy's name was, or they were using Twitter to question the meaning of life or announcing to the world that I'd found a fantastic place for pizza.

But as soon as social media became a credible source for information, as soon as it became a search tool, and as soon as the major search engines started to notice and rank social media, I started to pay attention for my own business and for my clients.

At first, I was averse. Then skeptical. I was appalled at the idea of my employees using work time to connect with other people and text or tweet the details of their day. That seemed like a huge waste of company time, not to mention a waste of their personal time. I know most executives and managers *still feel this way.*

Today I'm A Believer! It all changed for me when we started aggressively testing social media for Findability. When every tweet and every blog posting and my Facebook profile and my LinkedIn account started getting ranked as another element of my company's Findability, that was when my eyes were opened to the fact that *visibility and activity means increased search engine ranking for Findability.*

Social Media and Search

We used to think that social media was one thing and search engines were another. That's no longer the case. LinkedIn, YouTube, Twitter, Facebook are all being watched and spidered by the search engines.

With the right use of keywords in SEO (Search Engine Optimization), PPC (Pay Per Click) and social media, you can achieve what I call *World Domination by Keyword Phrase.* You can dominate results in the search engines by using traditional Internet marketing and social media. You can't do it any more with traditional Internet marketing methods alone.

> If you are not familiar with these terms and concepts, get a copy of my first book, *The Findability Formula: The Easy, Non-Technical Approach to Search Engine Marketing* (available on Amazon or from *Findability.com*). It has everything you need to know—and more—about how to get found in the search engines through the use of the right keywords.

How Does *Findability* Work?

1. First, you get your own website ranked under your most important keyword terms. You make sure your content and keyword density and word counts and meta tags and title tags etc., etc., all support this effort so that your site achieves top rankings in the major search engines.

2. Next is Paid Search, also called Pay Per Click advertising or PPC. This is the way to buy placement on a search result page under your keyword terms. If you did your job right in 1. above, you now occupy *two* spots on the search results page for the keyword term you're after.

3. There are still eight or nine other spots on that first page. This is where social media comes in. If you play your social media cards right, and learn to use your keywords in your profiles and tweets and updates, then you're going to show up on that results page in yet another listing. You'll pop up three, four or five times on Page One. That's keyword dominance. And, like it or not, whoever ranks highest and/or most on Page One of a Google search gets the credibility, trust … and the business.

Visibility and Credibility on the Traditional Search Engines

Google has done a masterful job of making itself the authority in search. Consciously or unconsciously, searchers hold to the belief that, "*Whoever Google ranks as important, that's who I believe is important.*"

If a searcher sees your company on a page not once, not twice, but three times or more, that searcher is going to assign your company a high degree of credibility and trust. Chances are, yours is the result they're going to click on. Of course that's what you want, for all the obvious reasons and for one less obvious reason: The more the searcher sees your company, either as a tweet, YouTube video, blog or on your own website, you are the ONLY GAME IN TOWN and you significantly increase your chances of getting clicked. You have PUSHED your competitors off the page of that keyword phrase in search results, and you own as many of the potential search results as possible on page one. That's your goal.

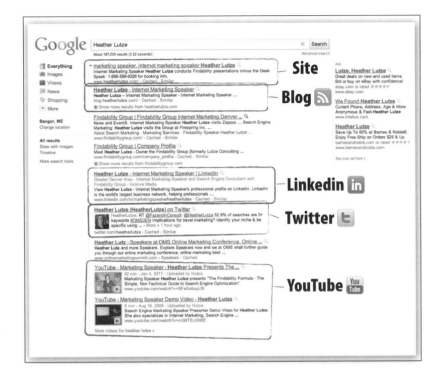

Visibility on Social Media Sites:
Social Media Sites ARE Search Engines

You're not just using social media to improve your visibility on traditional search engines. You also want to become findable on the social media sites themselves.

The social media sites—Twitter, Facebook, LinkedIn, and YouTube—are also search engines. People are doing business inside those search engines. They're communicating and sharing information in a way that websites don't.

People want social assurance—proof—that they should do business with you and your company. They want community input and encouragement from other people because they've grown skeptical of websites as reliable and trustworthy sources. They want real-time information, and they want it from someone ELSE besides YOU.

> If you're skillfully using your keywords on your Facebook profile and people are posting on your Wall in real time ... if your LinkedIn profile shows what you're doing NOW and where you're speaking ... if your Twitter page is awash with updates and comments ... all of these pages broadcast the *opposite* of static and stale.

Let's say you're thinking about getting some help with search marketing this year. You find The Findability Group in a search result and visit our website. It's hard for you to know how fresh that information is, how long ago I wrote my first book, what I'm doing now, what people think of me, or even if I'm still active in my industry or have been bypassed by newer, more cutting-edge thought leaders.

BUT ... if you see on my LinkedIn profile that I'm speaking to some big organizations in Washington DC this week and Philadelphia the following week; if a workshop attendee from San Francisco tweets that it's the most informative and understandable search workshop he's ever attended; and if you see a video of me doing a presentation on YouTube that was just posted on Tuesday, you're going to "get" the idea there's nothing stale about me or what I do.

It will be clear that I'm still active, vital, dynamic, that my expertise is still very much in demand, that clients and workshop participants and keynote audiences are appreciative enough to bother to post comments ... I'm a real person, current and not a robotic response.

That's the difference between a stagnant website and a vital, up-to-the-minute, dynamic presence on the social media sites.

Each of the tweets, LinkedIn and YouTube experiences mentioned are search engines unto themselves AND they also help my ranking on the traditional search engines. Your company is "findable" when prospects search inside of social media or on Google. You show up for them when they need you the most!

What about Employees?

Do I want my employees engaged in social media? You bet! Why? Because it's all about visibility. Every time one of them uses our company keywords on a social media site, it's another notch up in the climb. If my SEO Manager tweets that she's at a conference in Atlanta; if my client-care manager posts that we just delivered XYZ website on time and it's LIVE and looks great, that's NOT a waste of company time.

It is:

1. Sending a message about what we do, how trained we are, how skilled we are, how well delivered and yes, how cutting-edge we are; and
2. It's MORE VISIBILITY for the company. *More visibility means more business.*

*This is where social media goes beyond mindless chatter and moves into a **powerful business portal for your company**. And this is **why** you want to learn how to use social media.*

Demographics

If I haven't convinced you yet, it's probably because you're telling yourself that all this information might be interesting, but social media users are NOT your demographics. *Pew Internet* and the American Life Project report why you're wrong:

- *One in three adult American Internet users* is on a social media site.
- There are *647 million* searches on Facebook each month.
- The average age of users on LinkedIn is 41.
- Facebook's average age is 33.
- The average age of a Twitter user is 31. Not 14 … 31 years old!
- Social media is for adults, like you and me.

Truly Targeted Communications

Marketers, advertisers, branding experts, managers and executives talk a lot about an organization's *target market*, but companies often have more than one target market, and it's a challenge to have your marketing communications speak appropriately to each of them.

For example, your website is probably geared more toward prospects than to existing customers.

One of the great advantages of social media as a marketing tool is that you can direct different communications to different segments of your market. Think of your fans—those clients who love your company, your products and services. Isn't what you want to communicate to them different from what you want to say to someone who is just starting on their buying cycle; or someone in the initial stages of research; or who is just listening in on the conversation?

This is where *Crowd Sourcing* comes into play. Think of *Crowd Sourcing* as a huge party. You've invited everyone to come; they share a common Internet and each is willing to evangelize about your brand and products. It's the ultimate opt-in!

You can have all your existing clients in one group on Facebook. You can have another Facebook group that's dedicated to new and prospective buyers. And you can communicate differently with each.

You may want to give your loyal customers access to white papers, book recommendations or videos. You are creating and maintaining relationships in this medium, and in order to keep that vital, you want to keep your happy customers fed. Of course you would feed them very different information than the communication you would engage in with either a brand new customer or even a prospect that's just embarked on their buying process.

What you're doing with these very targeted communications is building *relationships*. Because when people feel you are speaking to them, they feel *important*, *connected*, *involved* and *engaged*.

Multi-Directional Communication

In addition to communicating differently to your different audiences, social media offers another—and perhaps most important—advantage: conversation and dialogue.

A traditional search engine, like Google, Yahoo! or Bing, is a one-way communication tool. A user types in a search term, gets results pages, clicks on an entry, and ends up on a website, which is another one-way communication. It's static. There's no interaction.

Social media sites, on the other hand, offer two-way, even multi-directional communication. People can post questions; they can engage in a dialogue or a group conversation. Anyone can listen in on the conversation and/or jump in at any time. It's a very different experience.

Imagine if you're considering the purchase of an assembly-required bookcase, a manufacturing software package to increase efficiencies on the plant floor, a pair of nurse's shoes, a hybrid car, an air conditioner, sales consulting services or a laptop. Now imagine that instead of just a web page touting the product or service, you could engage in a conversation with other users in addition to the manufacturer. You could read others' experiences, ask your questions, voice your concerns, get answers, and receive feedback, guidance and opinions. How much more inclined would you be to buy in this setting than in response to a static website where all you get is what the company says?

In this scenario, there's no longer just a company "telling" about itself, there's a whole community of people out there involved in a conversation. *A whole community.* This is key.

The Power of Community

Let's go back to the party with hundreds of guests. You asked the attendees to please raise their hands if they are interested in receiving ongoing information about your company's product or services over time. They all raise their hands. This is the power of a group or community.

NO more double Opt-In like emails or worries about spam filters; these people have voluntarily told you they are interested in being kept informed.

YES! This is truly what customer-focused marketing is all about. Tell me what I want, when I want it. Now that's personalization!

They want to make sure they're making the best decision with the right company at the best price. How do I know that? I ask my friends. I ask my community. I want you just to consider that this could be the turning point in your marketing programs. That social media, handled correctly and set up, can be highly productive, and that can open your business up to a world of prospects and warm leads like you've never imagined before.

Brand Management

Another big advantage of social media is brand reputation management. Social media sites are a great way to monitor the collective pulse of what people think and say about your company every day. As a leader in your organization, it is critical for you or your designee to stay on the edge— the cutting edge—of where your customers are. This is always important, but even more so in a recessionary economy.

With social media sites, you don't have to wonder what your public is saying about you and your products or services. And you don't have to pay for a survey or focus group in order to find out. It's all right there in the most public of forums—and it's an invaluable source of information and a golden opportunity. A new and upcoming position in Fortune 500 companies is the CLO: Chief Listening Officer. Are you listening?

Company Personality

Social media gives your company yet another extraordinary opportunity: the chance to create an online personality for your organization. Sure, your website, your collateral, your logo, even your corporate colors are part of your brand identity, but social media goes a step further and allows you to express a personality.

Whenever I speak on this topic, I notice a lot of executives scratching their heads or furrowing their brows. It's clear that many have never thought about what their company personality might be. Stoic, Professional, Fun, Quirky?

Beyond professionalism and competence, what personality would best represent the organization? **You.**

One of the things you will need to do before venturing into the world of social media is to figure out who you're going to be out there in this brave new world. Are you going to be fun, engaging and unexpected? Staid, conservative industry leaders? All business, all the time? Are you going to inject humor? Will you be all left, or right, brain? Creative? Edgy? Intimate? Personal? It's time to create your corporate persona.

Personality is often a difficult concept for corporations and usually warrants extensive conversation:

- Who do we, as a company, want to be in the arena of social media?
- How do we express an authentic and engaging personality that reflects who we are?
- Why would people want to be our followers/ friends/fans?
- Why would they care?
- What is it people really want to know and learn about us and from us when they engage with us through social media?

These questions are part of the process of embracing and then embarking on the social media journey to *greater visibility* and *deeper engagement* in your marketplace.

Two Corporate Stars Using Twitter ... Zappos and Comcast

Zappos: Putting the Best Shoe Forward

Zappos.com is an online shoe store. Well, they started as a shoe store. They've expanded into clothes and accessories now, but their core identity is still shoes. Zappos loves to have their customers come visit. If you go to Las Vegas and want to tour their facility, they will come pick you up at your hotel. They encourage visitors to take photos and videos. Many companies prohibit this. Zappos *wants* you to. They encourage visitors and customers to tweet about the tour, to blog about the visit. Their corporate culture is open, fun and inviting. They're proud of who they are, and they've got nothing to hide.

In this open, sharing and welcoming environment, Zappos makes it clear that their visitors and customers are appreciated. And they made that clear early on in their business model. Their corporate personality is easily extended to their social media profiles.

Zappos is one of Las Vegas' gems. Monthly, over 1,000 Zappos enthusiasts visit corporate headquarters. In 2010, I was presenting at a conference in Las Vegas. My friend Orvell Ray Wilson was also speaking at the same conference—we decided that we couldn't pass up a visit.

The next morning, the Zappos' SUV picked us up, as they do anyone who requests it, and we spent a delightful three hours—the energy was contagious. We were greeted by freshly popped popcorn and rock and roll music as we entered the tour area. We loved the personalities expressed throughout the tour—working there was anything but sterile. Both of us took a "seat" in the Throne Room—Zappos culture is that every customer is Royalty … there was no question in our minds that people loved working there as much as the customers loved ordering from them.

You can follow all of Zappos employees on *Twitter.Zappos.com* and see what's going on as a collective conversation of all of the employees and their social chatter. The website *Twitter.com/Zappos* is actually Zappos CEO, Tony Hsieh. It features his own profile and his comments about what is happening right now. At the time of publication, Zappos Twitter account had 1.7 million followers and growing.

He's a huge fan of social media and feels that companies should encourage their employees to use it with customers. In his interview with me, he says the following:

Whether it's with Twitter, Facebook, or whatever the next thing is, the easiest way to deal with everything is to just encourage employees to be real and use their best judgment.

Tony Hsieh is also actively setting a personality for his followers. Not a stuffy CEO but a friendly, approachable guy who just happens to run a billion dollar company. He's a real person, talking about his real life. It's very personal, and very engaging. His followers and fans love it—Zappos' bottom line reflects their enthusiasm.

It's not just fans of Zappos that has embraced the way Hsieh does business. *Search Engine Watch* reported:

Zappos + Twitter = Innovative Success!

Most companies use **Twitter** as a PR machine, covered in a thin veil of down-home personalization. But **Zappos'** CEO exposes a deep level of intimacy and behind-the-scenes information.

Tony Hsieh's book, *Delivering Happiness* goes deeply into his company vision. I highly recommend it to better understand how to capture your company's true personality. Read his interview at *Findability.com/Thumbonomics*.

Comcast: Reversing Communication Failure

People notoriously hated Comcast customer service. For years, Comcast was ranked #1 as the poorest in customer service categories across the board. In an effort to change the perception that Comcast was unreachable and unresponsive, it created a Twitter site called Comcast Cares (*Twitter.com/ComcastCares* or *@ComcastCares*). What Comcast achieved within this one site is a classic study in what social media can do to mend old ways and reinvent new ones.

Comcast Cares is a portal where customers can reach a real, live person 24/7.

Bill Gerth, known as Comcast Bill, tweets on this site with helpful messages, plus videos and conversations that are generated from customers' questions and complaints. Through this portal, customers can reach a human 24/7 and get assistance with problems and get their questions answered.

I was intrigued with the responses that came through the Comcast Cares portal and wondered if there were any changes within Comcast itself when it became apparent that the public was using it. Were there any specific changes within the "culture" of Comcast since the creation of Comcast Cares? In my interview with Bill Gerth, he responded:

> Social media is just one small aspect of the many exciting ways that Comcast is working to improve our customers' experiences. There's a lot of energy and excitement at Comcast around how we can transform the customer experience along with a renewed focus on putting the customer at the center of all we do. In fact, we've updated our company credo to reflect that and now offer the Comcast Customer Guarantee, which is our promise to hold ourselves accountable for providing a superior customer experience the first time, every time.

Comcast has grown and evolved so quickly over the past decade that our culture is continually evolving. The adoption of social media and the customer outreach from the DMO Team is representative of the overall evolution of Comcast from a regional cable provider to an innovative entertainment and communications service company.

Bill Gerth ✓

@comcastcares Philadelphia, PA

My name is Bill Gerth also known as @comcastbill. We are here to Make it Right for our customers.
William_Gerth@comcast.com
http://www.comcast.com

When a response is sent to the customer, a picture of the Comcast agent who is being interacted with is included. It's clear that Bill Gerth can't work 24/7 for Comcast … He's built a team of clones that can react and interact with each query that comes in. What's impressive is how each is totally on the ball.

Comcast Care's site is clean, has all their contact information and a REAL picture of Bill. Bill's mission statement on his profile is: *Make it Right for our customers.*

Comcast made a specific effort to have a fun, engaging, personable corporate personality on social media. There are more than 50,000 followers for Comcast Cares. That's 50,000 people who WANT to be part of the conversation with this previously despised corporate monolith that put customer service on hold, requiring them to punch through a series of numbers with robotic responses. Comcast today wants to be connected, in touch and engaged. With Bill Gerth's vision, this site has dramatically changed the perception of Comcast as a company.

comcastcares Bill Gerth
@shophiaholic Whats going on?
7 hours ago

comcastcares Bill Gerth
@spblowers Send me account phone number and i will look into
7 hours ago

Do you know when you are connecting to your customers and readers, really know? Bill Gerth found out when he made a posting that was non-business, merely a mention that it was his mother's birthday and he would be away from his computer for a few hours. I had asked him if he had had any "aha" moments using the Comcast-Cares portal. He shared:

One time, I had tweeted on a Saturday night that I would be away for awhile as I was celebrating my mom's birthday. I did mention I would be back later that evening and would respond once I returned. When I logged back on, I was surprised to see tweets of other customers trying to help each other and also saying, "Let Bill have tonight with his family." I was amazed and honored to have people reaching out trying to help some of our customers.

It's obvious that not only has Bill Gerth created an asset for Comcast, he's developed a Comcast Community, a fan club that every company would enjoy.

Risky?

Maybe the idea of a social media personality for your organization feels risky to you. Maybe you think that just being professional and trustworthy is all the "personality" you want your company to have.

But what's happening in the world today—perhaps as a result of social media and perhaps because social media is just facilitating this revolution—is that a whole new level of communication, transparency, authenticity, humanity and engagement in relationships is expected and demanded of organizations.

There's no more hiding behind the corporate veil. The people doing business with you, or considering doing business with you want to know who you are. The people "following" your company on Twitter and other social media expect a relationship. They expect real-time, authentic communication.

When smartphones entered everyday life, the Power of *Thumbonomics* was born. You cannot enter a workplace, coffee shop, restaurant, public environment, even your own home today, and not find someone receiving and sending messages on them. Electronic information is the new norm—newspapers and books are read and reservations are made electronically now—only to increase with time.

The mobility of the mobile world and your thumbs are the fingers that do all the walking today for gathering and sending information. Information that keeps you in your customer's eyes and thoughts. Being adaptable and learning the secrets of social media will fast-forward you and your company—it's amazing what technology has done for companies both seasoned and new at the gate. The understanding and savvy use of social media will make, or break, yours. Are you ready for the Revolution?

Thumbonomics is a road map and a guide for creating a successful (and authentic) social media personality for your company and then putting it out there in the social media universe … and get ready to reap the rewards.

You just finished this chapter. Congratulations! Now tell us what you think, the tools you use and get additional offers and giveaways. Scan this QR Code with your smartphone or go to *Findability.com/Thumbonomics1* for more Thumbonomics insights.

2

The Road Map

Your Easy Six-Step Marketing Program

When I sat down to write *Thumbonomics*, my objective was to give you a clear action plan to execute an effective social media marketing program for your organization. What follows is your six step "road map" that is detailed, practical, and best of all—simple to follow.

Step One: The Leadership Team Meeting

This important first step brings all your executives and brand managers on board. At this initial meeting, you will discuss the objectives of your social media program and address the fear around social media as well. (I wouldn't involve employees at this level, although they will play a significant role later on.) Get all your key leadership people in the room and really talk …

> OK, if we're going to do this, what return on investment do we need to get from it? What are the measurements we'll apply to track that return? What, exactly, is our goal, our purpose?

Did you know that social media marketing *has finite, measurable results*? Being clear about what you want from this project from the very beginning is essential to its success.

By the way, you'll probably find people in each department who are "social media savvy"; they already use it and really "get it." If your execs or managers are not in this category, have them bring someone to this meeting from their team who is. Most likely, that "someone" will have a Blackberry, iPhone or Droid and will have a Facebook app and a variety of other apps on his phone. Your "someone" will be virtually connected. Use the resources you have available internally and tap their social media expertise.

Step Two: Define Your Objectives

Each department in your organization will have different goals they would like to realize from a successful social media endeavor. HR, sales, IT, marketing, PR, and strategic leadership teams are all focused in different arenas. Make sure key department heads in each group are represented in this initial meeting.

The question on the table … How can each of those departments use social media to be more successful? What do *they* each need?

Each one will want something different from social media. They'll all have different programs throughout the year: different events for which they want to increase attendance; different products and brands they need to sell.

It's vital to include all these different department heads, right from the beginning, and get a clear list of two to three objectives for each group. Once everyone is on board, and the objectives are in place, ***you will be able to track their success using social media, and document it***.

Yes—you can make sure it's measurable, down to very specific results by department. How's that for an incentive?

Some questions to discuss:

- For targeted sales goals by product or service, should we use promo codes?
- What about contests?
- Can we do viral videos to produce the momentum that will get the results we're looking for?
- Do we create internal assets like white papers, videos, case studies we can re-purpose to use in our social media efforts?

What about the Big Picture?

Along with department-specific, finite number goals, you also need to talk about big picture goals for the entire organization. What might be some of your overall objectives?

- *Branding*: You want to brand the company as a whole, particularly if you are new or not widely known.
- *Reputation management*: You must be listening and monitoring what others are saying about your company and executives on social media. You need to make sure you are the first to know, not the last!
- *Thought leaders*: You want to be seen as a leader, an innovator, and a major player in your particular industry; putting out papers, information, videos and quotes.

- *Building customer relationships and retention*: This is one of social media's strong points. You also want to increase customer loyalty. How do you keep customers over an extended period of time? You need to keep feeding them. You need to keep giving them great incentives, and most importantly—keep communicating and touching base with them.

Let's take a closer look at this last one; it's a biggie ...

If I'm a friend of yours, I would call you for drinks or we'd get together for lunch or dinner. That's the way we would maintain a relationship. ***Think about maintaining relationships with your customers.*** What would you do to maintain that relationship over time? Send them thank you notes? Gift cards? How should you, as a company, address holidays or celebrations, an anniversary or birthday?

Obviously, you can't take all your customers out to lunch based on their location, but finding ways of treating your valued customers like your valued friends is key, and one of the things social media is terrific for.

Step Three: The Start-Up Committee

I suggest you create a small, start-up committee in your phase-one approach to social media. This group would consist of a few ***excited and savvy social media advocates*** within each department. Someone from HR, one or two from sales, IT, marketing, PR, and maybe other departments specific to your organization, such as your e-commerce group or graphic design group.

Excited and *Savvy* are the key criteria here …

I believe in this day and age you will find one or two people in every department, and they are not necessarily managers. I'm talking about people who are excited about social media; in fact, they're already on social media. They might be a bit younger than your management team, but the main thing is they are committed, enthusiastic, and really "get" the value of the different social media profiles.

If you, and your top executives, know nothing about social media, you are probably wondering who manages this smaller group of excited, enthusiastic social media evangelists?

Step Four:
Hiring a Social Media Brand Manager (SMBM)

Visit *Thumbonomics.com/Downloads* to receive a template of a social media job description that would be appropriate for this position.

A social media brand manager is a full-time, salaried position in your organization. You'll have to decide whether that's something you can afford now or perhaps see happening in six months to a year. You'll know, based on the size of your firm, whether a Social Media Brand Manager makes sense for your organization.

Are you shocked or dismayed by this step? Are you thinking, "I need another manager like I need a hole in my head?" Are you wondering, "What on earth will this person actually do?"

Responsibilities of the Social Media Brand Manager (SMBM)

1. Managing the social media committee, reporting directly to the executive team.
2. Setting up the metrics behind everything that's done in social media.
3. Working very closely with top-level management in each department involved in the social media program.
4. Automating the feedback coming from each of these departments.
5. Tracking followers, promo code redemptions, white-paper downloads, video views; in short—whatever is pertinent to feed success measurements back to those different, various departments.
6. Coordinating input from all departments. For instance, HR might feed available job opportunities or job descriptions; the sales department would feed promotions and sales initiatives for the coming year, or conferences they might be going to. Each department manager would contribute all pertinent information that could be made public to the SMBM. Their responsibility would be to make

sure it gets legal approval, executive leadership approval, and make sure it's consistent with the original measurements and goals established in that first leadership team meeting.

7. Monitoring all social media portals as well as having responsibility for using software that will keep them up to date. Then report all news related to each department accordingly, and create an appropriate response.

As you can see, a SMBM is actually a major, necessary position, if you are truly committed to having an effective and profitable social media presence online.

Step Five: Pick the Appropriate Portals

I recommend taking a look at all of the "big five": Twitter, YouTube, Facebook, LinkedIn, and blogs. They all have a place in your initial, right out-of-the-gate social media initiative. Please consider all of them in your initial push on social media.

To make this subject a bit more fun, we have developed a cast of "thumb" characters that represent each of the social media profiles for marketing your business. They will guide you through each chapter and put real business practices and ROI behind the jungle that is Social Media Marketing. Often, executives and managers see social media as the savages while they are the new explorers. Theirs is a new territory to explore with many dangers and issues they need to face. It's literally, a whole new world.

LinkedIn.com

LinkedIn is primarily for business-to-business communications. It's like a fancy country club where you dress up and use your best manners. Networking for business.

Demographics & Growth: See *Thumbonomics.com/LinkedIn*
Communication Method: Business-to-Business Communication and Networking Site
Business Application: Great site for targeting job titles, networking, job search and credibility in your field.
Slang: Networker, Applications, Recommendations

Facebook.com

Facebook is similar to the corner pub where people assemble to socialize, chat and share interests. Businesses now embrace the format where "everyone" is a friend.

Demographics & Growth: *Thumbonomics.com/Facebook*
Communication Method: Personal Profiles and Walls to post information
Business Application: Business/Fan Pages
Slang: Wall Posts, Pokes, Likes

Twitter.com

Twitter is short, sound bite type and spontaneous conversations you might have on a plane, subway, train or bus.

Demographics & Growth:
  Thumbonomics.com/Twitter
Communication Method: Tweets, Direct Messages, ReTweets, @ replies
Business Application: *Search.Twitter.com* is a search engine and people search for products & services based on key phrases in Twitter.
Slang: Twittersphere, Tweet Stream, Tweets, RT, DM, # (HashTags)

YouTube.com

YouTube enables you to create your own personal cable TV channel for free. Yes, production values DO matter.

Demographics & Growth:
  Thumbonomics.com/YouTube
Communication Method: Videos and Video Channels
Business Application: People use YouTube for an educational resource to learn and find useful "how to" videos when searching for services/products.
Slang: channel, embed code, views, subscribers

Blogging/RSS Feeds

Blogging becomes your personal soapbox, where you share opinions, information, and resources. Others can comment on your blogs, if you choose to allow them. Blogs and individual blog posts are:

Demographics & Growth: *Thumbonomics.com/Blogging*
Communication Method: blog posts and comments from readers
Business Application: Each blog post is indexable by search engines and blog subscribers receive an email notice with each blog post added.
Slang: URL: RSS (Real Simple Syndication), Comments, posts, blog roll, subscribers

As an organization, you have to decide if you can tackle all five. There are a lot of "second tier" social media engines as well that you might want to consider in phase two. But for this initial road-map, picking the appropriate profiles to start with is necessary.

How Do You Decide which Social Media Sites to Start With?

In the next few chapters, I'm going to walk you specifically through each one of the *Big Five*. We'll talk about how to use each one: its advantages, improving your Findability, and strategic recommendations to optimize each portal for the keywords that are important to your particular organization. We will also address how to track and monetize your investment in staff and resources to do this marketing correctly for results.

Again, I recommend getting into all five. But, you could also just pick one or two to start off, and then build out as you become more comfortable, or as you can afford to add personnel. If that's the approach you choose to take, I recommend Facebook first, then Twitter, LinkedIn, YouTube, and finally, blogging.

(Yes, blogging is considered a social media portal. In Chapter 11, *Blogging Findability*, we'll take an "in depth look" at how and why blogging could be one of the most important parts of your social media strategy.)

Step Six: Productivity Tool Selection

There are huge concerns around employee productivity and social media. If I've heard it once, I've heard it a thousand times from key executives:

> *I don't want employees spending all day on Twitter or Facebook.*

Understandably so …

One thing I've seen is that social media has all but replaced the water cooler conversation in many organizations. Think about it … Traditionally, you would grab your morning coffee, tea or soda, and stand around in the kitchen area chit-chatting about your projects with your co-workers.

That may still be happening to a certain extent, but what I'm seeing is that social media has taken "water cooler" conversation to a whole new level. We want to take advantage of that by leveraging social media productivity in a way that's meaningful for your organization.

What does that mean, exactly?

If employees are going to be on Facebook and Twitter; YouTube and LinkedIn, we want to make sure they're out there evangelizing your brand—not just talking about what they did over the weekend. Obviously, there is a time for personal conversation, and a time for talking about what they're doing in the organization, regardless of their position.

Wired magazine published an informative article in its February 2010 issue titled "Driven by Distraction." In it, Brendan I. Koerner wrote:

> In fact, regularly stepping back from the project at hand can be essential to success, and social networks are particularly well suited to stroking the creative mind.

The psychological benefits of having employees change modality in their daily tasks are an important and unexpected plus. Instead of hindering productivity, actively using social media during the work day can enhance it! After all, no one can be productive 100 percent of the time, without a break.

> Authorized access to social media gives your employees a way to share their expertise, find out how others might be doing it better, get up to speed on new developments in their fields, and engage with the group of people that they hold knowledgeable in their own fields.
> —Bernard I. Koerner, *Wired*, February 2010

Can you see the value in your staff accessing cutting edge information on how to do their jobs better? Or learning how to increase productivity? Perhaps someone needs to do a PowerPoint presentation, and they need resources and advice. Perhaps they need to quote statistics; they might need good, reliable resources in a certain area. Using social media could make all the difference in the world in regards to the quality and depth of someone's job performance.

When I was writing *The Findability Formula: The Easy, Non-Technical Approach to Search Engine Marketing*, I used LinkedIn extensively to get information from a vast group of people with search engine marketing expertise.

I asked, "OK, here's how I'm thinking about doing this particular task. How do you guys approach it? What have you found that makes it more efficient, lower risk, and gives a better output overall?"

Using this approach (known as *crowdsourcing*), I got a lot of different people in search engine marketing to give me their viewpoints on what they do, and was able to turn that into a really great source of recommendations for my own book.

Here's how this same idea can work for your employees:

Any employee can get bored or complacent with their daily activities. Perhaps they've done the same things the same way, forever. Opening social media portals gives your employees a set of resources they can use to make their jobs more productive, more interesting, and more engaging. The big bonus: it will help them to stay more excited about what they do every day.

I'll bet you never expected one of the benefits of a social media venture would be an increase in business creativity! Be prepared; it's actually going to increase excitement and enthusiasm when your people discover you are actually willing to trust them to evangelize for your company.

It Is a Huge Delegation of Trust ...

You trust them not to use the portal for personal reasons. Instead, to raise their level of responsibility and personal initiative on the job. That's big. Your employees will be thrilled to find you have set up a level of engagement that allows them to source from other industry experts, as well as their friends, all across the country, all around the world, to make their jobs more productive, more satisfying and more efficient.

These six key steps are essentials for social media success. They are your road map. Following them should dispel any staff objections along with any remaining fear surrounding social media. You will successfully establish clear objectives, measurements, and value regarding social media, from the top of your company on down. Your big picture objectives and individual department goals will keep you on track and moving forward.

Just like sexual harassment or bullying in the workplace, you MUST have a signed Social Media Policy in place for every employee given access to social media. You can visit *findability.com/social-media-coporate-policy* to get a template of how to start writing your social media corporate policy. This subject will be carefully described in Chapter 4, *Rules of Engagement*.

It's my hope that with this clear and simple road map to guide you, you'll take the leap of faith necessary to stay competitive in your own industry, become fearless in sharing what you do best, and allow your employees to grow, learn, and share what they do, to the total betterment of your organization.

Findability Makeover
Cleaning Out your Branding Closet
with Findability!

As a larger brand, you are probably investing a significant amount of your marketing budget in a diversified stream of advertising, including print, radio and television. But are you considering the offline to online equations in your marketing spend? Specifically, is the brand you are spending so much money to build being conveyed in your online presence?

TaxMasters (*txmstr.com*) is a tax resolution company with the slogan, "We Solve Your Tax Problems." When we first worked with them, they had recently gone public and needed to build their brand to new levels. TaxMasters spends a lot of money each week on marketing; advertising heavily on cable networks including *Fox News*, *CNN* and the *History Channel*, as well as on *Talking Points* with Bill O'Reilly, *The Dennis Miller Show* and other nationally syndicated talk shows.

However, is TaxMasters connecting customers from an offline commercial to an online search? For example, if I see a television commercial for "tax help" at 2 a.m. in the morning, and then get up the next morning to search online for that same help, how much am I really going to remember?

To maintain dominance in your industry, traditional offline marketing is only half of the equation. You must also be "findable" online under keywords people would remember long after they have experienced your offline offer.

For this makeover, I started thinking about marketing latency and how we could help TaxMasters make full use of their advertising dollars through Findability. TaxMasters was committed to helping continue the customer's path from TV ad to online webpage. To accomplish this, we took a look at *legacy paid search accounts* and Search Engine strategies, coming to the table with fresh, new ideas. Overall, we gave TaxMasters a Findability Score of 40, as they were dominant under some key terms, but needed more of a social media and blogging presence.

Problem: Offline and Online Brand Do NOT Match Up!

The online brand does not match the muscle or the magnitude of the television/print brand. If you are spending a significant amount of money on traditional marketing forums, it's important to give a consistent brand message as your user moves from an offline forum to an online search.

Lacking Findability can damage your brand because it's not consistent with what your potential customers just saw offline. You seem disingenuous and you lose customers to more "findable" competitors.

Action Plan: Clean the Dust Bunnies Out of Your Marketing!

We recommended an overhaul and clean-up of online marketing initiatives to support offline dominance. Specifically, when a customer sees a television ad, they should easily be able to "find" TaxMasters' online presence, no matter what "tax problem" keyword they type in the Search Engine.

The following three components will be outlined below:

Clean House in Pay Per Click (PPC)—Connect the TV branding with keyword searches in PPC, as well as continue the branding message using the Content Network in Google Adwords.

Get Found in Search Engines with Blog Posts—Experts blog, and blogs rank. Each blog post is a new opportunity to rank, and TaxMasters needs to take advantage of this power.

Pay Attention to Social Media—Consumers don't just search in Google and Yahoo!; treat all social media sites like you would a Search Engine.

Add Offline Branding Keywords into Pay Per Click Campaigns

- **Connect with Customers:** TaxMasters needs to be aware that people often search for services they see in TV ads, as well as try to "find" the ad online. If they cannot remember the company name from the commercial, they may revert to the actual show they were watching. (For example, by searching *"Tax Commercial Bill O'Reilly show."*)

  It is essential that their Pay Per Click (PPC) campaign be updated with keywords reflecting the names of all television shows that air their commercials, as well as the hosts' names and terms like "TV commercial," "tax help," "tax problems," and, "we solve your tax problems" (the TaxMasters slogan). Your television advertising may change over time, and Pay Per Click can quickly adapt and help you stay front-and-center for consumers who might search using the television show they just watched. (For more information about PPC campaigns—their structure and how they work— see my book, *The Findability Formula*.)

- **Establish the Brand:** The Google Adwords Content Network is often a very under-utilized part of a PPC campaign. Advertising on the content network allows your company to run ads on popular websites that may be associated with your product and/or service. If you are making a brand statement by advertising on national television, you should make the same brand statement by advertising on national websites. This can help cement your company in the minds of your searchers.

Make Your Blog Work Harder ... Each Post Ranks!

- **Be an Expert:** Blogging is an important element to help establish any brand, large or small, online. Consumers love reading blogs and learning important information about your industry. However, when you are a larger brand, your customers expect you to provide expert content and advice on your field.

If you truly are the expert at solving tax problems, then it is critical you provide information relating to solving tax problems including resources and strategies. Otherwise, even a large and established brand runs the risk of being out-ranked by a smaller competitor trying to establish their voice online.

- **Connect with Your Customers:** Blogging is also an important way to connect with consumers who may have recently seen your advertisements, provide them with additional information, and lead them on their path to purchase. Optimizing your website could take months; however, blogs can be written quickly and have the potential to rank quickly. This ensures you are connecting with the customers looking for you in connection with your ad.

Treat Social Media Like a Search Engine

Twitter and LinkedIn are platforms where searchers expect to find industry leaders and services.

- **Use Social Media Icons:** TaxMasters needs to add social media icons to their TV messaging and their website. This encourages a viewer of a TV spot to start the process of getting to know them. You want to give your consumers options—have a question answered, watch a video, or follow TaxMasters as an industry leader. Then, when the consumer is ready to take the next step, TaxMasters will be the "top of mind" expert.

- **LinkedIn as a Search Engine:** There is a search box located at the top right hand corner in LinkedIn. Make sure your company connects with the keywords potential prospects may be searching. If you truly are the industry thought leader in your space, consumers expect you to rank #1.

    Tip: Use keywords in your profile and your updates to be Findable under your core business keywords. (See example below.)

- *Search.Twitter.com*: Potential consumers are buzzing day-in and day-out on Twitter. Whether they are trying to find out, "What was the name of that company advertising tax services last night?" or, "Does anyone know a good Tax Problem-solving company?" it's important to participate in the conversation. Consistent use of keywords in their tweets will enable *search.twitter.com* to help TaxMasters to be found under terms like "tax problem resolution," or "tax help," but these keywords *must* be present in their tweets *all the time* to be findable.

TaxMasters' Results

1. Pay Per Click

By adding hand-picked sites as part of their content network, TaxMasters was able to increase their conversions from **99** in January 2009 to **244** in January 2010. That's almost a 300 percent increase in conversions—just by paying closer attention to the content sites. They also received a nice boost in traffic by deleting the content sites that were not tax or financially related and being more picky in general about which content sites were displaying their PPC ads.

2. Blogging

Experts blog, and blogs rank. Check out *BestTaxMasters.com/about*. By having a page on their blog that features all the television commercial ads they run, they can easily connect visually and keyword-wise with their potential customers.

Another Great Example of Success

Under a keyword search "TV Commercial Dennis Miller," I see TaxMasters Blog as #2 organic listing. This connects the offline and online brand the searcher expected, and continues him on his path toward becoming a customer.

Visibility and repetition are key in social media strategies. TaxMasters has engaged successfully in both.

3. Social Media Marketing

TaxMasters has gone full throttle into social media to "own their brand." They actively use keywords in blog posts as well as support their TV efforts with a great online search experience. TaxMasters has become a strong voice in social media by using keywords.

If you type in "tax help," the first LinkedIn search result is Patrick Cox, Founder and President of TaxMasters. As a public company, TaxMasters must keep pushing their branding envelope and own their brand 100 percent offline and online.

I look forward to seeing TaxMasters up their game online in the coming year and continue to dominate "tax" search queries.

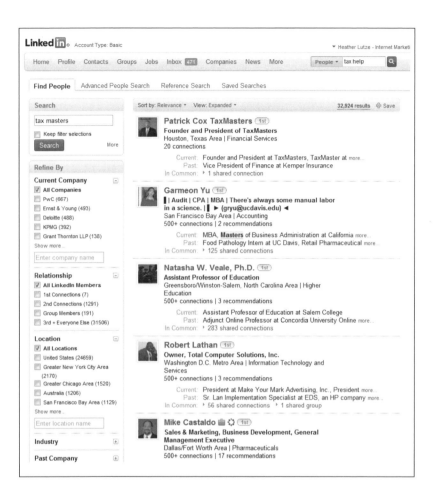

You just finished this chapter. Congratulations! Now tell us what you think, the tools you use and get additional offers and giveaways. Scan this QR Code with your smartphone or go to *Findability.com/Thumbonomics2* for more Thumbonomics insights.

3

The Fear Factor

Adapt or Die ... Your Choice!

In every area of business, the corporations I'm currently speaking with are in an evaluation period about using social media. Their question: "Should we or shouldn't we?"

Corporate legal teams as well as the older demographic among the leadership are frequently crippled by fear. If this is where your company is at regarding using social media, you are not alone. Honestly, I'm seeing it across the board. This *fear factor* is what's keeping companies from really opening into social media in a meaningful way.

Let's identify these fears; fracture the myths that fuel them; and create a break through strategy ...

Are Any of These Social Media Fears Keeping You Up at Night?

- *Employees*: How will getting involved with social media affect their productivity? What if our employees share something inappropriate over the net? What if they give away corporate intelligence, intellectual property—or worse yet, our company's recipe for "secret sauce"?

- *Security Issues*: What happens if we open up our firewall to these social media profiles? Does the IT department know the protocols to open up those portals *without jeopardizing internal databases and internal systems?*

- *Legal Nightmares*: Are we liable for anything any employee puts out there? What about false claims? Are we liable for those?

And yes—these are huge, legitimate concerns for any company. And there's still more. …

What information might be shared online, for all the world to see? There is no way to predict it, or control it.

If we have an exuberant employee who shares too much, or a disgruntled employee who knows too much, could that jeopardize our internal processes and procedures? We don't want to reveal the magic that makes us who we are and makes us so successful.

And of course, the bottom line has to be considered— what resources will it take to build a whole new department to handle a social media program?

What about Our Reputation?

Perhaps the biggest fear for most companies is reputation management. Here's the problem: every organization, in any type of business, will occasionally have unhappy customers. We all know that no matter how hard we try, it's impossible to have 100 percent customer satisfaction.

What about that one person who is disgruntled or upset with your product? Of course, he/she is the one who turns out to be savvy with social media. This is what could happen:

He posts nasty reviews all over the net …
He sets up a Facebook profile saying your
    company sucks …
He even launches a site called *YourCompanySucks.com.*

There are people who really will make it their life's work to ruin your brand. It has happened. But, avoiding social media will do nothing to solve the problem.

Using Social Media Can Actually Enhance Your Reputation

After working with many companies having these kinds of issues, I can assure you it's really difficult to push these disgruntled consumers off the search results page— *once they rank above your corporate brand.* This is a huge concern for many companies, and legitimately so. Trying to fix this kind of attack on your company's reputation is a nightmare.

But, although using social media will not prevent unhappy customers, it can give you a proactive approach that will keep you dominating the search results under your name.

If Someone Searches Your Brand, This Is What You Want Them to See on the Search Results Page:

- Your paid ad (PPC)
- Your corporate website (*OurCompany.com*)
- Your blog (*blog.OurCompany.com*)
- Your Facebook page (*Facebook.com/OurCompany*)

- Your YouTube channel (*YouTube.com/OurCompany*)
- Your LinkedIn (*Linkedin.com/OurCompany*)
- Your Tweets and Twitter Account (*Twitter.com/OurCompany*)

"Why Have All Those Sites, You Ask ...?"

Because now, *you've taken up almost all ten spots on the search result page of Google, Yahoo!, and Bing.* Customers searching for you will see everything you have to offer, instead of websites trashing your organization. There are other benefits to thoroughly owning a search page as well.

If someone is upset with you and wants to complain online, they will discover that you have a customer service Facebook page, you allow and even encourage public feedback, and you are actively, aggressively working with your customers to make sure they stay satisfied. Instead of posting independently, they will wind up joining in the conversation about your brand. Surprisingly, you may have far more "happy" customers offsetting any negatives!

I know you have your fears and hesitation about social marketing; my fear for your organization is simply this:

If you don't engage in social media, you're missing out on an opportunity to protect your brand and its reputation.

Look at the Bigger Picture

My recommendation to companies who are fearful about getting into social media is ...

Embrace social media and walk through the fear.

I'm going to walk you through the whole process, and *make it easy.* I'll show you how to minimize your risk and include tactical strategies to make sure your organization stays protected and ahead of the competition.

If you distrust the whole idea of using social media, could it be because you don't really "get" how it works? You have no roadmap; you simply don't know how to start, and then, where it will lead?

Thumbonomics will give everyone in your leadership team and management teams a clear, step-by-step understanding of how it works. It will present a phased approach to social media, starting off with a lower risk policy, wherein you open it up to a smaller group initially. Then as you become comfortable, (and see the benefits!) you'll open up to a larger group.

The First Step ...

Deciding you are going to give social media a chance may just be your best shot to take your company to its next level. Take the plunge. Move into the 21st Century!

Talk to your leadership team about their fears; from the president on down. What are their biggest concerns with social media? Is there anything that could be reducing productivity because social media is not being used? Is there anything that is keeping them up at night that involves the use or nonuse of social media?

If there is, you might discover what's keeping them up at night is fear of what your competitors are doing.

And I'm here to tell you—*every day you don't set up social media (because of fear) is another day you've given to your competitors to be at least one step ahead of you.* You are literally handing the competition the advantage!

If they embrace social media before you do, they will start stealing your clients away from you—and right onto *their Fan pages, their Twitter accounts, and their YouTube channels*.

Findability Makeover
Dealing with Findability Disaster

As business owners, it is rare to completely satisfy every client, every time.

However, these days if one customer gets upset they have myriad Internet sites to express their discontent. One of the worst cases I have seen was a disgruntled former employee who blasted a company after they were fired. Imagine searching for your company name and finding a scathing Yelp review from an employee you just let go. Your next thought might be, "Where else?"

Now with plenty of free time, that ex-employee makes it his life's work to "stick it to the man." I can tell you, you have not experienced panic until your website is ranking next to *RipOffReport.com* or a similar site loaded with brutal reviews. I have spent my entire career helping people be found on the Internet; now I want to address the topic of how not to be found. The question is, when ugly content is posted, what can you as a business owner actually do?

My response is to strike back, but with an attack of "goodness" and happy customers! Yes, use sugar, not vinegar to push them off the page. (My mom would be so proud.)

Problem

Someone on the Internet does not like your company. You are seeing a rise in negative reviews on *Yelp, Google Local* and *RipoffReport.com*. How do you plan a counter attack to push them off the search results page?

Action Plan

Start by looking rationally at this problem with a plan of attack that does not include calling in a "favor" or hiring an expensive lawyer. There is a much faster and safer way to address the problem.

Displace the disgruntled with positive, happy customers—therefore knocking the naysayers off the results page. Most companies have tons of happy customers; it's always the one percent of unhappy customers on whom we tend to focus.

As the old adage goes, "A happy customer tells one friend, an unhappy customer tells ten." The following five steps will be outlined in detail below:

1. Secure your company profiles on review sites.
2. Optimize your profiles, making sure data is accurate and up-to-date.
3. Actively request positive feedback from happy customers.
4. Setup and capture all brand names in social media portals.
5. Watch the negative reviews drop down and surround profiles with happy customer reviews.

Step 1: Grab Your Company's Brand Profiles and Secure Them

Find your company on major review sites that actively rank in search engines like *Yelp.com, Places.Google.com, Local.Yahoo.com, Citysearch.com*, etc.

Secure the account on record with the review website and identify yourself as the official business owner. Lock it down with your correct information. It is never pretty when a competitor or disgruntled customer takes the account before you get around to capturing it.

Complete the profiles as much as possible, paying particular attention to detailing your customer service policies and disputing resolution records. Link to your Better Business Bureau rating, if possible. Make sure to add your customer service hotline or link to a page that addresses customer issues.

Step 2: Optimize Your Review Site Profiles for Findability

For a good user experience, include your target keyword phrases in the following areas: Title, Company Description, Promotions and "Other."

Make sure to use keywords in your profile like "Television Repair Denver CO," or "Family Medicine La Jolla CA." This elevates your profiles inside the review site, when searchers are really digging to validate their purchasing decision. They want the real skinny on your services, your products and past customer experiences. Ranking highly inside the review sites helps validate buying decisions when customers are in the final shopping stages.

Step 3: Actively Fill Reviews with Positive Feedback from Happy Customers Initially

Reach out to your most loyal customers, explain the circumstances and politely request they help you combat this very negative review. You will get many customers who will immediately jump at the chance to help you.

Next, if you have a physical store location, instruct your employees to ask customers to write a review on *Yelp.com* or *Places.Google.com*. Then, tell them that if they provide proof of the review, you will have a small gift for them.

Coupons for discounts or $5 Starbucks Gift Cards make great thank-yous.

Record an extra message on your business voicemail to actively campaign for reviews. This may sound something like:

> Please post a review on *Yelp.com* or *Citysearch.com* and receive a little gift for your appreciation! Thank you for your business and helping us to serve you and the community better.

Step 4: Set Up, Capture and Monitor Your Company's Brand on Social Media

Companies often forget where their happy and unhappy customers communicate. Social media sites are a great place to commiserate with others about good and bad experiences.

Make sure to set up, actively monitor and participate in your company's presence on *Twitter, Facebook* and *YouTube*.

Use free tools such as *Alerts.Google.com* and *Tweetbeep.com* to keep track of what people are saying about your company and brand so you can respond accordingly. If you have the budget to monitor your online reputation, consider sources like *Radian6, Buzzlogic* and *Nielsen.*

Step 5: Watch Negative Reviews Fall and Happy Customers Speak for Your Company

As you capture your social media accounts under your company name and fill review sites with happy customers, the negative review will be surrounded by positive commentary. You have killed the negativity with kindness!

When you optimize your profiles with your company name and keyword phrases, you will start to fill the search results pages under your company name. You now "own" every search result when someone searches for your business. If a negative review is posted on *RipOffReport.com* or another review site and ranks under your name, it is surrounded by a resounding number of happy customer reviews.

As business owners, we probably will never think it's okay to have an unhappy customer. But it's important to always be prepared for them. In today's social Internet community, the voice of an individual can have long-term, detrimental effects on the brand and profitability of your company.

Be prepared to fight back by asking for help from your loyal customers who know the truth about your company. It has been my experience that loyal customers will jump through hoops to help you.

Rule of Thumb

Your social media savvy competitors will pull your loyal customers into their fold, because they are building a personality which is not based on fear. Rather, they're building a personality based on open communication, transparency, cutting-edge marketing and ability to change with the times.

All that, simply by embracing these amazing social media sites and daring to utilize the vibrant, open communication they provide.

Your job as an executive or manager is to *dispel the **fear factor*** in every area, and lead the way. Make the decision as a corporation that you are going to embrace social media, and watch what happens.

You just finished this chapter. Congratulations! Now tell us what you think, the tools you use and get additional offers and giveaways. Scan this QR Code with your smartphone or go to *Findability.com/Thumbonomics3* for more Thumbonomics insights.

4

The Rules of Engagement

What's Communicating Got to Do with Your Company Online?

Everything!

A crucial part of any social media endeavor is setting up clear, concise rules of engagement for everyone involved. Doing this will ease any last worries you may have about your employees getting involved and communicating about your organization online.

Start with a small subcommittee, including key people from different departments—ones who are truly excited about social media. Once that subcommittee is in place, the next task is to set up the actual rules governing their participation inside of social media.

It's time to create a *Social Media Marketing Policy*, one specific to your organization's needs. Here's a link to the online social media template:

Findability.com/Thumbonomics/socialmediapolicy

This is the same one I give to all of our clients, containing an outline of what should be in this corporate policy.

What Is a Social Media Policy and Why Do We Need One?

It's vital to have a written policy, stating employee guidelines and rules for using all of your social media platforms. You might start with a policy that's specific to your small social media subcommittee, because they'll be out there right away, hopefully on Twitter, Facebook, LinkedIn and YouTube.

This initial group, along with your social media brand manager, will help to write the rules of engagement for the entire company. It might be six months to a year until you open up those profiles to your entire company. By then, I guarantee you will have learned a lot and will be confident that you are doing the right thing …

A social media corporate policy should indicate what type of content is—and is not—OK to Tweet or post on any social media site during business hours. For example:

- If someone has had a bad day at work, or is upset with their boss, it's completely inappropriate to Tweet or Facebook about that.
- If anyone discloses any specific corporate intelligence that has been clearly outlined to them—that could be grounds for termination.
- If anyone bullies or sexually harasses another employee during office hours through Facebook or Twitter, that would be grounds for termination.

You'd think this would be obvious, but it must be made very clear to everyone which type of content is appropriate and pertinent to your social media objectives, and which type of content is pure misuse of these profiles. The rules need to be very specific, based on each individual company. Laying it all out plainly, in a written document, is vital to the success of this project.

Everyone in your organization who participates in social media profiles for your company **must sign this document**. It will be placed in their HR folders—only then can they be allowed to participate online.

Coming up with your firm's specific rules of engagement is essential for your peace of mind.

It's one of the things that make this program so safe and effective. When your social media policy has been drafted, run it by legal. You want to be covered, legally speaking, if something happens. Despite rules, policies, and training, there is no way of knowing what people may say or do—you need to be covered for that.

If you have your social media brand manager on staff by now, one of his main responsibilities at this stage will be setting up this social media policy, always focusing on what's most important to your organization.

He/she will assign platforms to the different departments. Perhaps different platforms will be more relevant to different departments. Facebook might be a more effective platform for one department, and Twitter or YouTube more effective for a different department.

Once you've got your social media marketing policy down, we'll move into actually working with the major social media portals. Here's how you'll start ...

Reserve and Hold

I want you to *reserve* and *hold* all your core brand names on Twitter, LinkedIn, YouTube, and Facebook. When I say *reserve* and *hold*, I mean:

- Set up new accounts with your corporate name. These will be your "official sites."
- Also set up accounts for any key brand names that you wish to hold, or at least *squat* on. You may not intend on *holding* or using these accounts forever, but you need to make sure that your brand has captured and reserved all of your brand names, or potential brand names, for your own purposes.

When the Findability Group worked with Goof Off, they hadn't secured their website and discovered that it was taken. We had to use *GoofOffStainRemover.com*. Within a short period of time, they were no longer lost, they were found. They were now findable under "Goof Off" their brand name as well as the problem it solves, namely, "Stain Remover."

The moral is: secure everything is soon as you have an inkling in your eye (include your name and products)—

URL, Facebook, Twitter, LinkedIn, and YouTube. You can always drop it if you don't use or want it. But you can't claim it if someone else steps up and takes it.

Hold and *squat* applies to names that are negative as well. We all want to have *MyCompanyRocks*, but do you want to own *MyCompanySucks*? Yes, you do! In a form of a pre-emptive strike, gather up variations that someone unhappy might use in a future date. The cost to you is nothing but time in passing now—a task that doesn't take long. For the future, it could be priceless. Think of it as a now-or-never scenario.

Just as car license plates can be personalized in the form of a vanity license, so can URLs for Facebook, Twitter Linkedin and YouTube.

Gather Up Rogue Accounts

Once you have reserved all your corporate names on the social media platforms we're recommending—Facebook, Twitter, YouTube, and LinkedIn—it's time to find out just what is already out there about your organization. You might be surprised …

If you search your corporate name on Twitter, Facebook or LinkedIn, you might find accounts that have been set up by former employees, or fans of your company. We call these *rogue profiles* or *rogue accounts*. Mail from these accounts may be swirling around in someone's inbox, but no one seems to know where they came from, or who set them up.

Send out an email to everyone in your organization, asking if they know anything about these accounts. Even if no one knows anything, you will still be able to either take control of them, or remove them. In this chapter, *you'll find links for the dispute centers at each of the social media sites.* You can file a formal complaint or petition to the owners of an account for which you cannot find the passwords and user names. (By the way, this is quite common.)

It's also possible that "outsiders" have set up accounts pertaining to your company. This can be good news, as well as bad news. When BP Oil was headline news in 2010 after the explosion of one of their offshore rigs, there were a variety of URLs and social media accounts set up whose objective was to gather and deliver negative news. The more they posted, the more they dominated key placements in Google, Bing and Yahoo!

You might have fans that have set up rogue profiles. (Consider yourself lucky!) You might have people who are passionate evangelists for your brand. (How wonderful!) These are customers who love your product. However, those may be rogue accounts that you cannot acquire.

Since these rogue accounts are set up by fans, and are entirely positive, then what is the problem?

One of my clients had a huge number of evangelists; literally thousands of people who just worship them. As a result, there were entire communities of people who had set up, "official" sites about this company—*that were not official at all.* An official site is one that you, as a corporation, claim as your own. Make sure you state within your description on your profile that you are the official site.

Here's my recommendation …

Every account you set up, on any social media platform, should have the word, "Official," in the title or profile description if possible. I believe Facebook is the only social media site that doesn't allow the word "official" in the account name.

You want people online to know what is and isn't official. You want them to know whether they are communicating directly with you or with someone else. Otherwise, it will be confusing to people who want to join *your groups*. They want to follow *you* on Twitter. They want to follow *you* or recommend *you* on LinkedIn. Use "official" in your profile descriptions as well as the account name if the social media site will allow you to do so, if not, include in your profile and content. This is a must for Facebook.

Frequently the public cannot tell the difference between your official page, and all of these rogue accounts that are out there. By adding as much info about your company as possible will help users determine if the page is actually official or not. Links to your site, and photos, are great.

It's important to gather up as many rogue accounts as you can. To find them, simply do some extensive searches inside the social media portals. Remember that each has their own internal "search" feature. Begin by putting in your name and variations of it. It's important to be fully aware of what's out there regarding your organization. Put together a list of all rogue accounts that are discovered.

It's a terrific policy to contact them, and let them know you truly appreciate what they're doing for you. (If you feel like any of these fans are really representing your brand, they might be a candidate for your social media brand manager position. They're already out there working hard for you—you might just want to make them a job offer.)

If there are lots of people already talking about you on social media, you might find a lot of rogue accounts. Be prepared to fight for the ones that are truly yours, or anything that says *Official*. You may not have to always acquire all of these Fan pages. Reach out to each and ask them to link to the official page: "For more info, check out the Official Company Fan Page."

An excellent example of this is when we started working with *Parelli Natural Horsemanship*. They had no social media at all and had not captured their brand on any of the major social media portals. There were rogue accounts by many of their loyal fans some with the word "official" in the titles as well. We set up their profiles and were able to capture their brand as well as the names of Pat and Linda Parelli, the founders of *Parelli Natural Horsemanship*.

Parelli now has an entire department of five at the time of *Thumbonomics'* publication, dedicated to the communication and support of their loyal customers and fans on Twitter, YouTube, Facebook and blogging. The door was literally going to burst open with people who wanted to evangelize their brand for them. Parelli was able to capture them and wrangle them together to work to extend their notoriety in social media. They have now launched *Parelli Connect* for their horse membership community. It's a combination of Twitter and Facebook for horse lovers. Brilliant! Visit *ParelliNaturalHorseTraining.com* for more information.

Sometimes, while working on a social media project with a client, we've discovered amazing videos, testimonials and groups already set up, because people love their products and services. Can you imagine a better outcome?!

Establishing Your Company Personality

A major element in the rules of engagement is your online "voice." Hopefully, you've already established your personality as a company. You want to be perceived as gregarious, cutting edge, professional, thought leaders—whatever your corporate personality is.

Now you have to decide,
"What is our online voice going to be?"

To explain that, let me explain the difference between your "Person" and your "Persona." If you go out on the weekends and have cocktails with friends, you don't Tweet about that. That's personal. That's your person, your individual identity as a human being and not to be reported on company social media sites.

If your employees want to set up personal accounts on social media, they can take care of that on their own time. That's where they will Tweet about their holidays, their vacation plans or the amazing drink they had last night at this really cool new bar. That's their person, their out-of-office persona. We don't want that showing up on your corporate social media sites.

Instead, we want an *in-office* persona. Here's an example:

Here's my title: I am the director of marketing for My Company, Inc. These are my responsibilities. And here's what I do every day.

All of that info should be in their profile. Their profile photo should be extremely professional, perhaps showing them in a business capacity. It might be a picture of them sitting in their office, in front of their computer—whatever indicates a professional persona as the Director of Marketing for My Company, Inc.

All your key people involved in the project will set up their Twitter, their YouTube, and their Facebook accounts with their professional persona. Everything they post in that social media account must specifically pertain to what they do, day-to-day, in their job at My Company, Inc.

To repeat, no one is talking about what they did with the family over the weekend. They've totally separated their "person" and personal life from their professional "persona" as a business executive or employee within your company.

You may be wondering how tweeting about the day-to-day workings of someone's job adds to your company's voice. When employees share with others the nuances of what makes your culture work; the hiccups that they sometimes run into, and resolve; the support or encouragement of a manager; the excitement of a product; or even a company celebration or kudos from a customer; it all adds to your fabric with the general public—your growing fans.

For the HR Department, Social Media Opens Up a Whole New World ...

Another subject that needs to be mentioned is HR considerations, especially for your upper-level managers and hiring professionals in your organization.

There's been a lot of conversation within the social media marketing community about whether it's ethical or legal to check someone's Facebook profile when you're hiring them. Is it acceptable to follow them on Twitter? Make sure you understand the precedents and acceptable practices in hiring.

Legal—or not? You need to know. In an article on *Career builder.com*, it was revealed that over 20 percent of employers check out the social media status of potential employees. Many of the respondents reported that they hired based on the social media profile and one-third stated that they didn't hire after reviewing content. What were the deal breakers? Photos that were determined to be inappropriate or references to drinking or drug use.

Below are several resources you can use to find out what is legal in this regard: what government or HR precedents have already been established. It's critical for your management team to know what information you can and can't source for HR purposes, to protect your company.

Slow and Steady ...

Let's take stock of where we are. What I'm calling "the rules of engagement" is a two part approach. In Phase One, you started small.

- You started with attaining leadership agreement.
- You've set up the protocols and goals for the social media sites you plan to start out with.
- You've set up a subcommittee.
- You've created very clear rules of engagement for that group.

Once you've tested for three to six months, it's time for phase two—to open the program up to the entire company. By this point, you'll have gotten a feel for social media marketing, and learned many things. You'll know how busy your brand manager is and if he or she is overwhelmed and needs help. You'll have worked out the details of exactly what needs to be in your social media corporate policy.

I believe it's very important that you start slowly and not rush into phase two. There's a lot at stake here, so take the time to learn, and do this whole thing correctly. I have found that people who participate in social media are not very forgiving. If you open this up to them, you set all your profiles up, and you don't follow through, you've basically wasted all the time you spent setting it up and will never see good results. Your team has created a good marketing strategy that you just push aside and never use.

The number one glitch I see in corporations is that they get very excited initially. They're very, very enthusiastic right out of the gate. They get lots of momentum moving forward and seem truly committed to this kind of project— but then there's some disconnect somewhere, and the excitement wanes.

In the first six months, they have put a lot of energy into building out this social media, creating their voice, and then somehow it fades out. The people who are following these companies on Twitter and LinkedIn suddenly see the activity go from 100 percent to 10 percent. Suddenly, there is nothing for the followers to follow.

I am here to tell you, nothing frustrates your fans, friends and followers more than lack of communication. They opted in for info; they expect to receive it. You need to keep the momentum steady and paced. No one likes a fair weather friend—and the people who are invested and participating in social media are no different.

In the coming chapters you will receive the social media productivity tools you'll need to make this project sustainable over time. It seems to be human nature to have a lot of initial excitement, but not be able to sustain it.

If your original momentum starts to fade, you'll need some kind of shot in the arm to keep it going.

That might be the perfect time for phase two. By opening the program up to the entire company, you get a new injection of enthusiasm, and get everyone on board to make the program as successful as possible.

Zappo's Tony Hsieh has this to say on the subject of passion:

> In business, passion is what will get you through the difficult times. Also, your passion will rub off onto your employees, which will then affect your customers and business partners.

If you are the social media brand manager, you want the program to grow over time. Look for others who are running the social media programs in their organizations. Reach out to them; they can be an invaluable resource. Befriend those people; follow them on Twitter. As the person who is running the social media effort in your organization, staying connected with your peers through social media and utilizing it fully is an absolute must.

Rule of Thumb

The business world is morphing on a daily basis. In late 2000, the Emmy award-winning *Mad Men* was introduced on television. The men and women executives and support staff of New York's Madison Avenue exemplified the methodology of corporate campaigns of the past. Viewers and critics marveled at the authentic representation of what marketing and advertising was like just a few decades ago. In comparison, yesterday's product launches and corporate communications are dinosaurian compared to what is used today.

Your world cannot risk being dinosaurian. Communicating with your clients and customers has never been more critical. Using the Rules of Engagement and the how-tos of the chapters that follow will build you, your brand and your company bigger and stronger.

You just finished this chapter. Congratulations! Now tell us what you think, the tools you use and get additional offers and giveaways. Scan this QR Code with your smartphone or go to *Findability.com/Thumbonomics4* for more Thumbonomics insights.

5

Social Media Marketing
Keywords for Findability

It's in the Psyche of the Online Beholder

Grande, extra hot, skinny, non-fat, hazelnut latte with Splenda ...

Why am I telling you my personal Starbucks coffee order? And what do individualized coffee orders have to do with keywords and social media?

People use both regular search engines and social media search engines to find exactly what they want, exactly the way they want it. They expect the results to be personalized to them, just like their Starbucks coffee order.

If I order a grande, extra hot, skinny, non-fat, hazelnut latte—and all I get is coffee, I am not going to be happy or satisfied. I will take my business elsewhere. Likewise, the "coffee" approach to marketing on Twitter, Facebook, YouTube, LinkedIn, etc., is not a strategy that will work for you. You need to meet peoples' needs and allow them to find you *their way.*

When Al Franken, now a US Senator, was a regular on *Saturday Night Live*, he did a skit that perfectly illustrates the problem with how people approach social media. The character stands in front of a mirror and said, "I'm smart enough, and I'm pretty enough, and by gosh, people like me." Here's the link: *youtube.com/watch?v=NuGf34F0f5g.*

I think a lot of people believe this is what social media is, just talking to yourself; no one else listening. Unfortunately, social media is nothing more than talking to yourself in a mirror *if you make no effort to be found outside of your own personal or business profile.*

How do you make yourself "findable" on social media sites?

Simple—by strategically using keywords in everything you do. Yes, it will take some initial work, but you'll reap the benefits in a couple of different ways:

1. You'll be rewarded by your ranking in the search engines, because search engines are watching what's going on in social media. They're looking for key indicators to help them decide where to put you in search results.

   If you use specific keyword phrases in your tweets, your blog post titles, YouTube video titles, in Facebook or LinkedIn profiles, then you are effectively conveying a message to Google about how you want to be found.

2. Just like when a customer gives her order to a Starbucks barista, and receives her perfect beverage, when a user puts her keyword phrase into the search box in Twitter or Facebook, she will receive the perfect result—you! By using the highly personalized keywords, and using them correctly, all of a sudden, you and the searcher are brought together. You're no longer just talking to yourself in a mirror, you are making warm, meaningful connections with prospects that have indicated an interest and you can show them how to come up with a solution…your product or your service.

Effective use of keyword phrases puts you in touch with a viable user audience that you can connect with, you can help, and last but not least—*you can sell to.*

There's more to findability than social media. My entire first book, *The Findability Formula*, illustrates this keyword process. You will receive everything you need to be successful marketing on social media with this one book. To really understand what findability means outside of social media, perhaps to improve the page ranking of your website, I recommend you read *The Findability Formula* which is available in pBook (print) and eBook (electronic) formats, as well as DVD.

The Path to Purchase

In the fifth chapter of *The Findability Formula* I identified the path to purchase that buyers go through. Potential customers take directed actions as they move through the buying cycle. The first one might be *informational*. Informational keywords are the words like "coffee" and "chair."

The customer, at this stage, is just looking around; he's just starting the buying cycle. He hasn't yet decided who he might buy from. He doesn't know the key online retailers. He wants more information; perhaps checking out consumer reports and comparisons.

When he finds out the things he needs to know, he then moves on to *shopping*. At this point, the customer knows the specifics of what he's looking for.

- I'm looking for an ergonomic chair.
- I'm looking for Guatemalan coffee.

Now the customer will not type "chair" or "coffee" into the search engine; he will type in exactly what he wants. He'll start searching for purveyors selling Guatemalan coffee, or ergonomic chair companies.

When the customer is actually ready to buy, he wants to go out and get it right away. He knows he wants Guatemalan coffee, and knows he wants it organically grown. That calls for a very different kind of keyword than "coffee." At the purchasing stage, the customer will type in an even more specific keyword phrase, such as "organically grown Guatemalan coffee in Denver."

Another example of a *purchasing* keyword would be "ergonomic chair for computer programmer in Colorado."

That's how it works for the consumer. How does it work for you?

Let's say your company sells chairs. You may initially think, "I need to be in front of the search volume for "chair" because there are five million searches on the word for "chair" every single month. Prior to starting the Findability Group, I worked for Yahoo! Search Marketing doing their advertiser training across the country. This very boisterous lawyer shouted out that he personally bids on the word "sex" because of the millions of searches each month. He was a mesothelioma lawyer and he wanted to hedge his bets that a percentage of people searching for "sex"' were also searching for a lawyer to help them with a mesothelioma case.

Traditional marketing has trained us to think in these terms. We buy radio ads based on number of listeners or amount of drive time. We buy newspaper and magazine ads based on circulation numbers or subscribers.

Search engine marketing is completely the opposite of traditional marketing techniques.

When you consider "findability," whether it be in PPC, SEO or social media, instead of just hitting the biggest numbers, you need to be connecting with someone's Starbucks coffee order—meaning their specific, detailed personal needs. It won't do you any good to try connecting with them via the word "coffee" or "chair." Because those searches lack intent and focus, they keep adding keywords to their searches to get better and better results. Bidding on a word like "coffee," "chair" or "sex" is a huge waste of time and resources as is using them in social media content. How do you do that?

Some investigative work is required. You need to discover exactly how people search for your products and services; really think about the consumer's path to purchase, including all the "informational, shopping and purchasing" keywords.

Our job as marketers in social media—as well as in pay-per-click and SEO—is to really connect with our customers in a way that's meaningful to them, based on the keywords they just put into Google, into Facebook's search box or *search.twitter.com*.

Using those main keywords in your Facebook wall posts, your tweets, the title of your video—that is how you'll connect and *get real value and bottom line revenue for your business*. When you think about social media marketing, think about the customer's process, and remember that it's your job to be found in ways that are meaningful to that customer.

If you want me as your customer, you've got to speak to me. It's not enough anymore to speak to me as a coffee drinker; you've got to speak to me as my personal Starbucks order.

"Coffee" or "chair" are two great examples of what those of us in the business call "ego keywords." Why? Because if you search these basic words with any keyword research tool (like the Google AdWords Keyword Tool, or some of the other tools I'm going to give you), you will see these huge, huge numbers. Very appealing to the ego, very easy to convince yourself that those are the best words for your purposes, but not really useful for what we are trying to do—which is connect on a more specific, individualized level.

If you base your findability on a single keyword like "coffee" or "chair," that shows a total misunderstanding of how people use the internet to make their purchasing decisions. You need to base your findability on how the consumer tries to find you.

When I was training for Yahoo! search marketing, we repeatedly pulled up search statistics for the word "cooking." We pulled it up every single month for two years, all across the country. These were huge search numbers, as you can imagine. We'd see keywords like: "cooking with Gorgonzola cream sauce; cooking for the holidays; cooking standing rib roast."

That would be in the October through December time-frame. January, February, and March, you would see cooking searches totally change to: "nonfat, low-calorie cooking," or "Atkins cooking." A very different set of cooking keywords turned up, because the keyword used is always based on what a person needs at any given time or seasonally.

When you're starting to do your keyword research, you need to understand the buying cycle and focus on the shopping and purchasing keywords; the part of the process when people make buying decisions.

- That's the point at which people join Facebook groups.
- That's when they'll follow you on Twitter.
- And that's when they're really interested in that sub-section of whatever you have to offer that speaks exactly to their personal needs; their own individualized Starbucks coffee order.

How Do You Choose Your Optimum Keywords?

I recommend developing a list of 30 keywords. Here's the best possible place you can find these all important words— in the page search campaign or Pay Per Click campaign you are already running. Simply pull the 30 or 50 top performing keywords out of that campaign, and make a list.

If you already know your keywords or from Google Analytics or another tracking tool that you have for your website, use them. Add your organic keywords to the list. These should be keyword phrases; two to three words in length are ideal for the shopping and purchasing part of the cycle.

One of my *go-to tools* is the Google AdWords keyword tool. ***Go to www.Google.com. Search for "Google External Keyword Tool".*** Click on first search result.

This tool allows you to peek inside Google, and see the amount of searches for a particular keyword in the last 30 days, as well as an average of the last 12 months, both globally and locally.

Step 1: Check the Psyche of the Searcher

LSIKeywords.com

LSIKeywords.com is a website that helps you:

- Reveal how often and where a Key Phrase is being used in the top search engine results.
- Expose every sentence, titles, headlines, images-alt tags, Meta-Keywords and Meta-Descriptions.
- Discovers opportunities when you find pages that are not optimized for any given key phrase.

In other words, you can connect with how the searcher and the search engine see the top website pages. Your goal is to use those similar keywords in your social media and mobile apps. You have now stacked the cards in your favor and are creating content with keyword phrases search engines are already ranking on page one.

This is the "neuro" search thinking your client is already taking when they look for a product or service in a search engine. Once you have generated your list in *LSIKeywords.com*, cut and paste the three keyword phrases into *Wordle.net*. Keep this list handy as you will need it for Step Two below.

Step Two: The Visual Representation of How People Search by Keyword Phrase

Wordle.net creates two-dimensional images:

A word cloud is a great way to create a visual representation of the keyword that is searched. The result displays a visual variety of your words ranging in size of importance. Print the image and keep it around you. Share a copy with your employees and associates to remind them of what the potential customer thinks of your products and services. It will keep them centered in their effort at all times when creating content.

Step 3: Check the Search Volume of Each Phrase

Now that you have discovered how searchers think about your product or service, make sure it's worth using in your social media content. Open the Google Keyword Tool *(adwords.google.com/select/KeywordToolExternal)* and check the keyword phrases you chose in LSIKeywords.com as well as any new keywords that present themselves as interesting in the Google Keyword Tool.

Sort through the keywords that are appropriate to your company and create a list of the ones you would love to use to connect with customers. If there are many searches for "organically grown Guatemalan coffee," and one of your products is "high quality Guatemalan organic coffee," then that's an excellent keyword for you as well. However, you might discover many other keyword phrases that are an even better fit, with higher search numbers. Try to choose keyword phrases that get over 250 searches per month.

Once you have your final list of keywords and phrases, start incorporating them in all of your Twitter tweets. Every time you do a video to post on YouTube, check the keyword tool and make sure that you name the video with a highly searched keyword.

Otherwise, quite frankly, you're just sitting there talking to yourself in a mirror. You may be doing interesting posts and videos, but you'll never manage to connect with a viable search community that could buy from you.

Other Useful Tools ...

1. *Google Insights* (*google.com/insights/search/#*). This is a wonderful trending tool that will give you great suggestions in regard to trends and issues that people may be talking about and wanting to follow. (With Google Insights for Search, you can compare search volume patterns across specific regions, categories, time frames and properties.)

2. *Ads.YouTube.com/keyword_tool*. This tool tells you what keywords people are using when searching for videos on YouTube, which can be a great resource if you're looking to title your videos.

3. *Search.Twitter.com*. This site will give you an idea of how people are searching and what keywords others are using in their tweets. If you use "organically grown Guatemalan coffee" in your tweet and someone types in "Guatemalan coffee" or "buy Guatemalan coffee," your tweet will show up, allowing you to become part of their consideration process by showing up in search results.

4. *Hashtags.org*. This site shows you the trending using hashtags all over Twitter. (Because Twitter provided no easy way to group tweets or add extra data, the Twitter community came up with their own way: hashtags.

A hashtag is similar to other web tags—it helps add tweets to a category. Hashtags have the pound symbol (#) preceding the tag. Hashtags are a simple and unique way to track trending, and for people to aggregate their conversations. Example: *#GetFound*.

Chapter 8. *Twitter Findability*, offers examples of using hashtags.

Pre-tweeting and the extensive use of the Internet, word of mouth was word-of-mouth. Now it's word-of-thumb! Imagine what branding buzz can be created for you when others begin to circulate in seconds to hundreds, even thousands of contacts? Thumbonomics has changed the way companies do business.

Social media is not a fad, it's the trend.

Findability Makeover
Revealing True Findability

What is "Findability" and how do you, as a website owner and Internet professional, manage and promote your site in a way that ensures those most interested are able to connect with and buy from you?

It should come as no surprise that those businesses most likely to fail on the Web have neither a firm set of online business objectives or an understanding of their online customers and what those users find most valuable. To prepare your website and business for discovery by consumers on the Internet, it is essential to possess a deep understanding of your business and its role in the lives of those consumers.

Below is an interview where *Web Site Magazine* interviewed me on my thoughts shortly after my book, *The Findability Formula*, was released:

WM: Where should a website and business owner begin; and what type of questions should he be asking?

HL: When looking at taking on a Findability project, a great question to ask yourself is, "Why?" What are you looking to accomplish through this initiative? What are your business goals and sales objectives? How about your expansion plans or exit strategy?

These are vital to the health and well-being of your enterprise over the long term. Having a concrete set of objectives for your Findability program allows you to prioritize initiatives, create a strategy based on your high-value outcomes, and keep your team aligned throughout the project. Knowing the answer to those questions will aid in the online positioning of your business today and prepare you for success tomorrow.

WM: What are some organizational clues that a marketing department or individual would be better suited to one particular channel when optimizing for Findability?

HL: A great source of success "clues" is to look at the history of your previous marketing initiatives and ask yourself what was effective and ineffective in those projects—and why. Companies may find that social media platforms, traditionally, have not been successful for their business, however, search engine optimization with long-tail terms are a better fit. Long-tail terms are defined as keyword phrases that consist of between two and five words, usually used when searching for a specific item.

This may mean that applying your long-tail terms to your social media platforms will be an effective approach. Conversely, if you are finding that your social media platforms are thriving, but your website is not, this is your cue to give more opportunities for users to act and interact with your website.

WM: What, in your opinion, is the biggest factor in search engine optimization success?

HL: It all starts and ends with links. The number and quality of inbound links pointing to a website is the most important determining factor in your online success. While crawl-ability and relevant content can certainly help position your site, it is the links that ultimately matter most. To gain links, however, a formal content strategy needs to be in place. For this reason, hosting a weblog on your own domain and optimizing the content on product and services pages really positions your content to receive those high-value links.

WM: Based on your experience, what type of content tends to attract the most links?
HL: Destination matters and content is everything. The quality of your website (the destination) determines the quality and quantity of the inbound links you earn. Creating, developing and promoting high-quality content pages that give users the information they are looking for is how you can get those links. Some things to remember are to keep it easy and simple, bullet points are great, and don't just use text—consumers love visuals. Of course, easy navigation, transparency about your company and an attractive design all play a role in delivering a great experience for your user.

WM: Is it true that meta data no longer matters for SEO?
HL: No … While providing meta-information on individual pages is far less important today than in years past, there is still a good reason to include this data—why let search engines define your content when you can influence what is returned on the search results pages? Your entire site also needs to be

organized in a way that does not interfere with search engines crawling the content pages. More optimized pages will not necessarily guarantee first-page rankings for a brand name or under core products and service lines, but it will get you a good amount of the way there.

WM: How should a business owner approach social media?

HL: Social media platforms can be a very powerful tool for your business. However, it is no longer enough to just "set up shop" on Facebook, Twitter, LinkedIn, YouTube or My-Space—you also need to optimize those channels. To ensure Findability, these platforms must be optimized with high-value keywords and managed on a regular basis. Dedication to active participation is a must for any business looking to start a social media program.

WM: Is there an optimal way to measure social media performance?

HL: It all comes down to the objectives you outlined before you began your campaigns. The great thing about the Internet is the ability to measure a tremendous breadth of metrics. Your optimal tools for measuring social media performance will depend on what you consider "social media success."

If you are looking to product sales and website form-fills as success metrics, Google Analytics can give great data. If you are looking for clicks to determine what is resonating on platforms like Twitter, tools like HootSuite (*hootsuite.com*) are great resources. If you want to track how big your following is growing, then resources such as Twitterholic are great tools. Essentially, if it's valuable to you, there is a tool to measure it.

WM: What is your biggest takeaway for businesses looking to take on Findability?
HL: The more pieces of this Findability puzzle that exist, the greater the opportunity for consumer discovery. For example, if your goal is lead generation, the ideal scenario is to have PPC driving pre-qualified leads to your website, your website optimized to get in front of your target search audience and actively involved in a social media community. Keep in mind, the concept of Findability really transcends search engines—we are talking about making your company as findable as possible to your online target audience. Sometimes that may be a search engine, other times that may be a social media community or even a press release.

Even if you have a SEO, PPC and social media program, it is your responsibility to continually get in front of your consumers online, wherever they are looking for you.

Rule of Thumb

Optimum Keywords will become a key element in your branding and marketing efforts. By using the same "search" tools that others use in discovering you, your company and its products via the Internet, you will be fast-forwarding your visibility and success.

You just finished this chapter. Congratulations! Now tell us what you think, the tools you use and get additional offers and giveaways. Scan this QR Code with your smartphone or go to *Findability.com/Thumbonomics5* for more Thumbonomics insights.

6

"The Big Five" Optimization

Ignore Them at Your Peril

I hear it all the time ...

You know what? I think Twitter is ridiculous. I don't get it. And I don't want to use it.

I would rather walk around a department store in my underwear than tweet!—(Real Quote from a conference attendee).

Isn't Facebook for teenagers? We're not going on there; I don't see the point.

Every time I've looked at LinkedIn, people write about a trip or meeting they are going on or returned from, or someone is now connected with someone else—I don't have time for this.

What my staff does NOT need is to watch TV during the workday—I don't want them on YouTube.

Blogging is just another time waster. I need my people doing their work.

Of course, you are entitled to your opinion. But, here's the problem with these objections. These social media sites may not be your personal preference, but they definitely are other people's preferences. We're talking huge numbers of people here, including your prospects—your customers. There are more than 800 million using Facebook alone. Huge numbers!

Watch out—this is where ego creeps in, especially for a marketer or manufacturer who doesn't "get" social media. Suddenly, you're standing in judgment of your customers' preferences, and as a result, seriously limiting the ways in which you are willing to be found.

The hallmark of a really good marketer is to
make sure you are everywhere.

———————

You could be findable by every single portal out there, if you so choose. Think about that for a moment—if I search for you by keyword phrase, or your brand or service on YouTube—you're there via a video that is usually just a few minutes in length.

If I search for you on LinkedIn—you're there, along with the written information on your profile that only you supplied, not someone else.

If I looked at Twitter, I would find short messages—ahas, insights, and recommendations—from you.

If I discover you on Facebook, especially a fan page that you've created, I can get additional insights of you and your company that could draw me into your circle.

Your tweets on Twitter could actually stimulate a break-through in a project that I might be working on, as much as a Blogging post could!

Think about how that could expand your options, your findability, and your potential growth. Please don't judge or limit the ways other people choose to get their information. (Certainly not if you want to be as successful as you could be ...)

Everyone has a different comfort level and different preferences in how they communicate. It's important to be mindful of that, because you need to be everywhere your clients expect to find you. Everywhere.

Charlie Cole, VP of Online Marketing for Lucky Brand Jeans reveals:

We have our website, our Facebook, our Twitter, our YouTube Channel ... We push our content into **multi-channels** because we know that users behave different ways, depending on the medium that they interact with. We want to make sure that **we're everywhere**.

We want to meld these two ideas: We want social media to be a **revenue driver** and we want it to be profitable, but we also want it to be this bastion of our brand. How can it **reflect the brand**?

Make no mistake—in this day and age people EXPECT to find you on …

The "Top Five" Portals: Blogging, YouTube, Facebook, Twitter and LinkedIn

Here's a brief rundown of each one, in order of importance to your social media program. Let's start with blogging.

1. Blogging

 This modality appeals to people who love reading, love new content and RSS feeds. (An RSS feed allows any new content to show up automatically on a subscriber's homepage or in their email.)

 I subscribe to Seth Godin's blog (*SethGodin. typepad.com*). Do you know Seth? He is a best-selling author who has been called, "America's Greatest Marketer." Each day, I get the latest post to his blog, containing a little tidbit of information about where he's going, what's on his mind, or what he's working on.

As a fellow marketing professional, I like to stay in touch with other marketing thought leaders, and I find his blog brilliant. I enjoy following him and what he's up to, and yes—I really do read every word of it. For me, reading blogs is one of my preferred methods of learning and finding new ideas and information.

Blogging is terrific for those of your customers who like content, like to read, like to know the details, want to get to know YOU, and like to be the first to hear what's new or what's on the horizon for your organization.

Blogging has a second important benefit: If you put one of your high value keywords in the title, Google will also love that blog, and index it very quickly. Search engines find blogs to be highly trustworthy resources. Within the vast sea of stale and unchanging websites, blogs tend to be much more current and extremely content-worthy for Google to rank.

Prior to Twitter arriving on the scene, many blogs tended to be lengthy—for some, they were full-blown articles. The short, 140 character microblog, has influenced other formats. Now, it is typical to find blogs of fewer than 200 words—not characters—but certainly shorter than the 800 to 1000 word blogs that were common in the beginning.

Blogs enable you to post pictures and videos with short keyword-optimized descriptions. If your company is going to share a video, write a post about the video and send the link out to your blog, (not your YouTube channel) where viewers can find information about you and post comments, if you allow them.

2. YouTube

YouTube is the new way to present information. It's video, as opposed to text; something that people really like. Many people are visually based, that's how they learn, and that's what makes the most lasting impression. Videos are instant gratification based.

Have you recently sent someone a really cool video?

Lucky Jeans has their own YouTube channel. They recently collaborated with designer John Robshaw, famous for his block printing. Charlie Cole adds:

> On one particular day, we're going to link to John's blog and his website. The next day we're going to **link to one of John's YouTube videos** on the art of block printing; one that shows him in action. Instead of placing it on Facebook, we're going to **link back to our YouTube channel**, and give fans the idea, again, to access us through **a different medium**, a different area, show them somewhere else they know they can find us.

The main objections to using YouTube run along the lines of the following:

- I don't understand video.
- I'm not a professional videographer.

- What would we make a video of?
- I don't have a YouTube channel.

If you have never done video, I can tell you—with today's technology, it's really simple. Using YouTube couldn't be easier ...

A couple of years ago, I bought a Kodak Zi8 high definition video camera and just started taking videos. I didn't try to create a "Steven Spielberg moment;" I simply made the videos easy and spontaneous. I use video to capture special moments—perhaps people coming out of speaking events, or getting ready for events.

How about videos of product how-to's, new product launches, or people simply using and having fun with your product? A client of ours who sells *heat guns* had no idea what they would do a video on. Then they mentioned that a distributor used a heat gun to make a grilled cheese sandwich. Aha—perfect! What if they had a video contest amongst their distributors to cook with a heat gun? Instant personality and fun with a commercial, industrial product.

Videos for YouTube don't need to be glitzy, glamorous or heavily produced. You don't need to hire actors. You don't need big dramatic music or fancy screen credits. It's more about listening to your customers, working with what is already in front of you and adding some creativity and fun.

I'll go into the uses of video for your organization in more detail in Chapter 10, *YouTube Findability*.

3. Facebook

It is currently the number one social media portal. According to Pew Internet and American Life Project (*PewInternet.org*), "Sixty-five percent of adult internet users in the united states uses Social networks" That translates to 50 percent of all US Adults. With the biggest user base, Facebook will definitely be your biggest plug-in to consumers. Anyone with a business interest also creates a business page.

Charlie Cole has revitalized Lucky Jeans' reputation with Facebook …

Facebook in particular and social media in general, gives us an opportunity to **romance the consumer** and not hard sell them. We've grown from 20,000 fans to over 200,000 fans in less than a year.

Looking at our **Facebook wall** on a day-to-day basis you're probably going to see **positive comments**.

Even if you see a negative comment, you're going to see a response from us within a couple of hours saying, "Hey, give us an email at *Scott@LuckyBrandConcierge.com*," or, "Here's how we can solve your problem." It's now a **great success story** that the employees of the company take great pride in.

4. Twitter

Twitter is the portal growing the fastest in popularity. Is what's known as a "micro-blog," meaning very short, small snippets of information. It may not be the way you prefer to communicate—using only 140 characters at a time. There are huge numbers who thrive on these small, bite-sized communications. Face the fact—Twitter is hugely popular and getting bigger every day. As New Years arrived in 2011, over 9,000 tweets were sent out per second.

How does Lucky Jeans utilize Twitter? Charlie Cole offers a great example:

> We designated May 3 as *Ask Nico Day*. Nico is our resident denim designer; he's worked in denim mills, designing denim for 25 years ... What do you want to ask him? Go to Twitter and tweet to *@LuckyBrand* with your questions, and then he'll answer all of them tomorrow on Facebook.

5. LinkedIn

LinkedIn is a B2B portal, primarily for business executives and business networking. Personally, I find LinkedIn very helpful, and fantastic for lead generating. If someone searches you on LinkedIn, they're going to see a treasure trove of information about you.

They'll see your history, your favorite books, and personal recommendations from people who have worked with you in a variety of different capacities. Your blog and even your Tweets can be ported right onto your LinkedIn profile.

That's the "Big Five," in brief. Are you starting to see the potential here?

In the next five chapters, I'll walk you through each one in more detail, giving you the strategic advice you need to optimize them to meet your company's goals.

You'll learn exactly how to insert keywords and take advantage of all of the tools, tips and tricks within each portal. I'll show you how they work together. Not only will this increase your Findability, you'll start connecting with a massive search audience that will be truly meaningful to your business.

Findability Makeover
Social Media Advertising Strategy:
The Five Must-Have Social Media Profiles
for a Great Marketing Campaign

Everyday it's harder and harder for small business owners and advertisers to keep pace with all the social media platforms on the Internet. It started with the personal profile phenomenon; quickly evolved into video sharing profiles, and then the flood gates opened up. Now, Internet users have hundreds of social media platforms to consider.

Any marketer worth their salt knows the value of setting up a social media advertising campaign on these free platforms. However, with so many options and limited time, small business owners must have a strategic and targeted approach to social media advertising...

As such, I have developed a Social Media Advertising Formula, made up of the sites that all advertisers, website owners, and business owners must have in order to run a successful social media advertising campaign.

Social Media Advertising Formula

There are five essential platforms business owners must have in order to harness the potential of social advertising. Each platform plays a very specific role, and the combination of all five is what will take your social advertising campaign to the next level. There is a secret ingredient at play here as well—the formula calls for a touch of optimization on each platform.

Optimization allows your social media to work with your website and PPC campaigns (Pay Per Click) to dominate the first page of search engine results. Essentially, my formula will make you the only choice as far as the searcher and Google are concerned.

Social Advertising Element #1: Blog

If you only have the time or desire to create one social media platform, a blog should be at the top of your list. Blogs give users a few distinctive advantages over the other platforms that make them absolutely invaluable in the world of Internet Marketing.

First, search engines love blogs. They have plenty of content and are easy for the spiders to crawl and categorize online.

Second, consumers love blogs. They aren't hard-sales, but rather a mix of marketing and education that online shoppers trust.

Third, every blog is a new opportunity for you to go after a new keyword. Whether you want to dominate a search page with one particular keyword or just have a presence under a different keyword, a blog is a free and easy way to get you there.

> **Directions:** As with a YouTube video, every blog is a new keyword opportunity. Use a keyword tool, and select your keyword before writing. Then, include your keyword in the title and throughout the content, but remember, never sacrifice consumer experience. Also, be advised that repeating a keyword too many times will show up as spam in the search engines.

Social Advertising Element #2: YouTube

The main video sharing platform, YouTube is one of the best forums available to create a viral marketing campaign. From publishing client video testimonials to creating social proof of your abilities, YouTube videos are a great way to get other site owners to link to your website.

Directions: Each new video is a new opportunity to optimize for a different keyword. For each video, be sure to include your keyword in the title and at least once in the description section. Feel free to subscribe to my YouTube channels (*HLutze* and *Thumbonomics*) to see examples of this.

Social Advertising Element #3: Facebook

As a closed community, Facebook does not rank in the search engines and makes the best choice if you want to have a personal profile online. However, optimizing your Facebook profile with your business keyword can make it an invaluable marketing effort.

Directions: Optimize your Facebook profile for one keyword and become the "go-to" expert in your industry for the more than 500 million Facebook users. Also, include some personal touches, but beware of putting too much personal information online. "Friend me" under *Heather Lutze* and *Findability Group* on Facebook to see this applied. I'll friend you back.

Social Advertising Element #4: Twitter

The latest, hottest rage, Twitter is a micro blog that limits posts to 140 characters. Although I typically hear the most skepticism about Twitter, it can be an amazing tool for your business. Twitter plug-ins allow you to update Twitter and literally push it out to your other platforms, such as Facebook. Additionally, Twitter posts rank in the search engines.

> **Directions:** Select one keyword and include that in all your Twitter posts. Also, don't forget to personalize your Twitter background for a totally unique and branded look and feel. For an example, follow me on Twitter (HeatherLutze).

Social Advertising Element #5: Linked In

A popular business profile site, LinkedIn ranks very well in search engines and is a great platform for sending event updates out to business associates.

> **Directions:** When optimizing your LinkedIn profile, select one core keyword (or search term you would like to be found under), use it frequently without sacrificing consumer experience, and watch your profile skyrocket in the search engines. Become my business associate on LinkedIn (Heather Lutze) to see how I have done this for my company.

With the combination of these five social advertising platforms, your online campaign is sure to be a success!

Rule of Thumb

As of this writing, Blogging, YouTube, Facebook, Twitter and LinkedIn are your Big Five. The rapid evolution of all things new on the Internet will deliver new portals that will jockey for "must use" positioning.

Thumbonomics and the Findability Group's team is constantly seeking and testing the new players as they emerge. Until any new portal becomes a major player under the social media guise, stick with the Big Five—none of them will disappear overnight.

To close, I asked Lucky's Charlie Cole, "What would be some advice you would give to other C-Suite executives about social media and what they might be missing out on if they don't fully engage?"

(continued)

His response:

"My advice would be, lighten up. I think a lot of big executives and a lot of large companies are scared to death about social media. Not getting involved because you're afraid of it is old world thought. You have to get involved now ..."

To read the rest of Charlie's fantastic interview, go to:

Findability.com/Thumbonomics

You just finished this chapter. Congratulations! Now tell us what you think, the tools you use and get additional offers and giveaways. Scan this QR Code with your smartphone or go to *Findability.com/Thumbonomics6* for more Thumbonomics insights.

7

Facebook Findability

Your New Marketing Window on the World

How would you like to have access to millions and millions of potential customers? Does that sound like a market that's worth your time?

Yes, there are over 750 million *active users* on Facebook—and 50 percent of them log in *every day (http://www.facebook.com/press/ info.php?statistics).* The average user has 130 friends. You'd have to agree, those are some pretty amazing statistics. Facebook's growth has been lightning fast; in fact, Mark Zuckerberg, the founder of Facebook was featured on the cover of *Wired* magazine with Bill

Gates and was selected as *Time's* Person of the Year in 2010!

I'm blown away not just by the numbers (which on their own would not mean anything) but by the *commitment level of Facebook users.* In any given major city, there are groups who routinely come together either in person or via the Internet to share and discover new ways to use Facebook.

While writing *Thumbonomics,* one day out for lunch, the woman behind the cash register noticed I had a microphone and tape recorder in my hand. (I originally dictated all these chapters, and then had them transcribed as the first draft for the book.)

"Oh, what are you doing with the recorder?" she asked.
"I'm writing a book on social media marketing
for businesses, using Facebook and YouTube,"
I replied, curious to see her reaction.
"Oh my gosh! I am *absolutely addicted to Facebook*."

Another example would be a friend of mine; she gave up Facebook for Lent! Now it's a very important part of her life and she sees it as a vice. She keeps Facebook up all day and sources it for all kinds of products, services and communications with work and friends.

Many devout users do become "addicted" to the high level of relevancy, connection and interpersonal communication they receive from actively engaging on Facebook. It's incredibly personable; quite different than any other connection on the Internet. I find Facebook revolutionary, not just for communicating with friends, but for *accessing business prospects as well.*

At its heart, Facebook lets people's lives matter one wall post at a time. My life matters in the bits and pieces I share on my wall and you reach out to your friends one post at a time. Pay attention to me ... my life has meaning ... I "like" you! There is some serious psychology operating here, and as business owners we need to know how to properly engage.

In the fall of 2011, Facebook reported:

- There are over **900 million objects that people interact with**, including Business pages, groups, events, and community pages.

- Their average user is connected to **80 Business pages (sometimes called community or fan pages), groups and events**.
- The average user creates **90 pieces of content** each month.
- More than **30 billion pieces of content** (web links, news stories, blog posts, notes, photo albums, etc.) are shared each month.
- The average user **spends 20 hours** a week.

I always liken sales to either dating or marriage. Marketing these days feels more like a date that "comes on" way to strong, and if you try to ask me to get married on the first date, then that's just CREEPY! This in its essence is why marketing is changing to a more social approach. The prospect decides when and where it gets its information; no one will "sell" to me before I am ready. When you connect with someone on Facebook, they are ready for the first date, i.e., to get to know your business. Is Facebook starting to sound more attractive as a business tool? Wouldn't you like it to be your content, about your organization—that is being so enthusiastically shared?

My company has had the pleasure of managing all of the social media and email for Keegan Gerhard who owns D Bar Desserts with his wife Lisa in Denver, Colorado. He is also one of three judges on the hugely popular Food Network shows *Challenge* and *Last Cake Standing*. I am a huge fan.

Jim Chan, Heather Lutze, Keegan Gerhard and Natalie Henley

Scan with smartphone to
see Keegan's video bio from
Food Network.

We sat down to talk about Facebook and how this has affected his business, his fans and his life. I began by observing that there is something unique and wonderful about his business. I asked, "What's a better way to get it across to a large audience?"

We have a mission statement at D Bar—we want to create a culinary sanctuary where you can relive old memories and create new ones. We want somehow to convey that D-Bar isn't just another milk and sugar shop. We need social media to convey that D Bar is special and here's how and here's why.

When D Bar first started to explore social media, they were excited, overwhelmed, confused and frustrated with all the possibilities Keegan reveals in Chapter 10, *YouTube Findability,* and at *Findability.com/Thumbonomics.* Just like so many, his biggest "aha" moment in using social media and Facebook came when he revealed:

I didn't understand how much people pay attention to what I do and say. I had no idea that people would ever care if I wrote a blog or I didn't.

I had to re-calibrate what I think about my opinion. I didn't realize people do care about it. They want to know about the challenges we face every day. There are some people who are trying to get a restaurant going … people who aren't on our level yet. I've discovered that posting our experiences and our challenges helps them; it's important.

By learning and implementing what works, and what doesn't, the use of social media has become an integral tool in D Bar's marketing strategy.

Setting Up Your Facebook Presence

Keegan Gerhard's Professional Facebook Profile

Scan with smartphone to go to Keegan's professional Facebook profile.

You want to make sure to capture your business name, initially. You want to use it as the basis for all your social media accounts.

When you set up your Facebook profile, remember—use your business persona. (Remember my discussion in a previous chapter on *person* vs. *persona*?)

Your goal is for your profile to look professional and represent you as a business person. Remember to use a photo of yourself in professional attire, preferably in a work environment. You might have your team holding your company logo or you can have a custom image designed with your logo, your picture and your other social media icons.

Do not use your logo, pets, kids or a cartoon. This is where your photograph should be—such as the one that was discussed in Chapter 4, *Rules of Engagement*. They call it "Facebook," not "Logobook." It drives me crazy when I see Facebook personal profiles using a logo instead of their picture. It's **Facebook**—use the clearest, most professional picture you have of you or your team. Personal pages are personal; business/fan pages are for business.

If you are the CEO of The Ultimate Chair Company, use a picture of you sitting in the nicest chair on your showroom floor.

When writing your profile, (or posting anything else online) you'll want to integrate the list of important keywords we talked about earlier. Hopefully, you've already done your homework in this area—see Chapter 5, *Social Media Marketing Keywords for Findability*. Out of that list of 30 to 50 keywords, know your personal top ten. These would be the ones you "would absolutely kill" to be found under by Google.

Keep this top ten list on a sticky note right on your monitor, and keep referencing these keyword phrases as you create your profile.

As the CEO of The Ultimate Chair Company, you'll put your job description and company description in your profile, mentioning that you run the number one ergonomic computer chair company in America. Now you've got "ergonomic" and "computer chair" right there in your profile.

That's one example of how to blend in your keywords. Use your top ten keywords throughout your profile. Remember, not only do Facebook users search inside the site; Google is watching public profiles as well.

Important: Under the privacy settings, make sure you choose the "Everyone" setting. In this way, your Facebook profile and anything else you post is public, it's accessible via the Internet and it's spiderable by Google.

You need to create both a business profile, and a business page (also called a fan page).

Your organization's business page is different than your personal, business profile. A fan page is all about the business you own or work for. Not you, but the business.

When you set up your fan page, it's OK to use your logo. I still recommend a photo over a logo, (with social media, the more personable the better) but if you have a great logo that you really love, you could use it here. Or, as I mentioned earlier, use a photo of your entire team holding the company logo or something creative that shows your company personality.

> The point of the Business page is pretty obvious—you use it to build fans of your business. Your social media brand manager's job is to build brand and notoriety.

Does all this feel too much to you? Are you wondering if anyone is out there who will really care enough to read your Business (fan) page? D Bar's Keegan Gerhard discovered just how much people pay attention to what he does and says.

> I had no idea that people would ever care if I wrote a blog or I didn't. I was surprised to find that if I say I'm going to write and I don't, people get upset. People are very vocal about it. "Why didn't you do this?"

So like Keegan, on your personal profile, you would post about things you're doing as an executive in the company; your travels, your speaking engagements, etc. Anything about the business itself goes on the business page.

I'm the front person of my company. It's my face on my books, websites, and business cards. People often get to know me by seeing me speak. I'm not a celebrity, by any means, but people know me because they've seen me speak or read my first book, *The Findability Formula*. They identify with me as a person first, and with my business second.

On my business profile, I'll post all the things *I'm personally doing* for the business— whether it be speaking, traveling, writing a new book, or whatever. This morning I tweeted about being in the studio today making this recording. For something my business is doing—for instance, if we take on new clients, write new web papers, create new videos—I post that on my Business Fan page, so that over time, I build fans of my business.

In my case, it has to be that way, because people tend to meet me first, before they ever come in contact with The Findability Group. If you have a business without a front person—as a manager or executive of the company, you would still set up both a business profile, and a business fan page.

To attract fans, add constant, interesting, relevant updates, not 100 percent company promotional. Include Free Stuff to Facebook followers only: discussions and contests, specials, sales, events the company is hosting, any kind of insider info that followers can't get anywhere else. This adds to your corporate persona and your followers will embrace it!

Here's another way Keegan Gerhard uses his Facebook page:

> I think the point of social media—yeah, it's entertainment, yeah it's connection, but beyond that—it's business networking at its highest level. If you post your problem or concern, or a frustration on Facebook—20 people answer right back with a solution from their experience. I want to both contribute to that and to grow from that.

Fantastic Facebook Features

You can and should customize as much as possible on your Business Fan page.

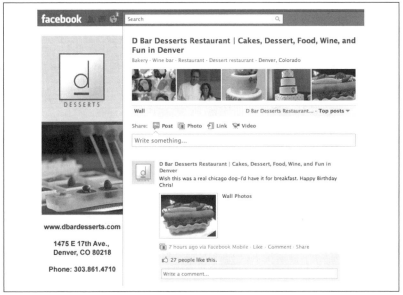

Keegan Gerhard's Professional Business Page

Scan with your smartphone to go to Keegan's Facebook business fan page.

Here are some ideas …

- Like Use the "Like" feature. When I "like" a fan page (which is simply done by hitting the "like" button at the top of the page), I am automatically added to the fan base of that page. The power of "like" is huge and is already transcending Facebook and you are seeing it on websites, blogs and videos.

  If I posted "I love The Ultimate Chair Company" on The Ultimate Chair Company's Business page, it would not show up on everyone's wall or newsfeed. Business page posts from followers of the company will never show up on other follower's profiles; they stay on the company homepage. If the *company* posts something on their Business page, it *will* show up on all of the Followers Newsfeeds.

  Another bonus is that Facebook has stats in the admin menus for how many page impressions each post has made.

- During the set-up of your Business Fan page, you'll have the opportunity to add a "Like Box" to your site and give people an easy way to discover and follow your Business page. *Always do it to your company site.*
- Identify the Applications link. Facebook Applications will give you the ability to feed other sources into your Facebook page. The idea is to make your company's Business page look up to the minute, super active—a mega cutting edge page—without needing to constantly be working on it.
- The first thing to do in Applications is set up what's called "a blog application" or a "blog feed." If you have a blog, it will take every blog post and post it on your Facebook wall.
- Another terrific application is SlideShare. SlideShare lets you take PowerPoint and keynote presentations and upload them for public viewing. If you want to be seen as a thought leader in your space, slide share can help you spread the word. Remember to use a keyword phrase in your slide title too.
- Facebook also has a **Twitter** application, so you'll also be able to import your tweets right onto your fan page. A word of caution: if you use this feature, look closely at the quality, and quantity of tweets. Too many may look like spam to your followers. If the quality is perceived as "low content," you end up filling your page with unimportant events.

There is a caveat about Facebook. If you talk to enough Facebook users, it's not uncommon to pick up some grumbling outside of kudos ... Facebook is notorious for switching features around. The good news is that new ones are added. The bad news is that sometimes it deletes a favorite. Go with the flow and learn to adjust as Facebook finds its way and grows over time.

A great example of how feeding your tweets into your Facebook can have huge impact is when I was recently in Mexico on vacation. I'd set up a bunch of Tweets in advance, for instance:

"Drinking Corona on the beach."

"Can't wait to get back to work. Yeah, just kidding."

This was to let people know I was out of the office, in a very professional, yet fun way that was appropriate to the circumstances.

To my surprise, several friends posted on my Facebook wall in response—they were upset with me because they thought I was spending time posting during my vacation. In fact, I didn't post at all. Twitter has some automated features. I had pre-written those Tweets to feed from Twitter to my Facebook account by using a feature of *Hootsuite*, an automated tool for managing social media communication. (See Chapter 4, *Rules of Engagement,* for a full explanation of productivity tools like *Hootsuite.com.*)

All of these applications provide a way to make your Facebook pages look extremely relevant and fresh. But at the same time, business appropriate and professional.

I set my page up using various applications, so I don't have to continually go on Facebook updating these profiles every minute of the day, every single day—who has the time? For business, that would be impractical, and not what we are aiming for. Instead, I'm suggesting customizing your pages in a way that makes them look continually updated— and you can get back to work.

Facebook Ads for Demographic Profiling

Recently several clients reported an increase in responses when incorporating Facebook ads over Google. Obviously, any ads you place should incorporate your list of keywords or phrases ...

Your ads can be targeted in various different ways, using demographic profiling.

Would it appeal to you to show your ad specifically to people of a certain age? Who speak a certain language? Only on their birthdays? Or how about only if they're engaged, or married, or divorced?

How would you like to get your ad in front of a Facebook user, based on the keywords they used in their profile setup?

You could also show ads to people based on specific locations, likes and interests, or by education and type of work they do. You can even say, "I'd like to market to anyone who's a friend of Steve Jobs" or, "… to anyone who's a fan of Apple iPad, a smartphone group."

Yes, ads on Facebook can be targeted that specifically! For more info, go to *Facebook.com/Advertising*.

Scan to learn more about Facebook advertising.

Marketing to specific target groups can be very, very successful. We've been testing this for a while at The Findability Group and have gotten some extremely exciting results with Facebook ads by tightly focusing on demographic profiling.

I hope these tips have given you a way to optimize your Facebook profiles in a way that will be meaningful for your business.

What's Your Findability?

The Findability Formula | Search

The Easy, Non-Technical Approach to
Search Engine Marketing
Heather Lutze

Findability Formula: The Easy, Non-Technical Approach to Search Engine Marketing is a must have book for every web site owner.

Remember; always stick to your business persona ...

Stay professional ...

Stay credible ...

And use those applications or plug-ins so your profile always looks up to date, even though you won't be online every minute of the day, or even every day.

Findability Makeover
Expand Your Business by Thinking Global, but Acting Local

Many small business owners think that in order to be successful, they must dominate the world. After all, their product is just as good for people in Ohio as in Nebraska.

But often, the real business is right under your nose—right in your own backyard.

Understanding the nuances of how to attract and capture a local search audience and convert them into paying clients is a big challenge. Fortunately, you can increase your Findability, dominate web search results, and attract new customers right in your own hometown.

The question is, how do you succeed in a local market where competition is fierce and your company offers the same perceived product or service as everyone else does in the area? How do you achieve a real competitive edge in a localized market? Often, it's about two key things:

- Getting Social
- Getting Local

If you want to stand out in your local market and increase your web ranking, the following are some key ways to get social, get local, and get a whole lot of business.

Get Social

Social Media Marketing is an excellent tool in an Internet Marketer's toolkit. It gives you a great opportunity to demonstrate how your company is different, and it gives a real voice to your online presence. Many businesses that do some social media marketing do a good job of helping consumers find their social media platforms off the main website. And, for the most part, they do keep their accounts updated with relevant, high-value information. However, in order to really harness the potential of these platforms, you need to make a few changes with a localized spin that will go a long way for search engine marketing.

Tip #1: Get Everyone ... and Everything ... on the Same Page

Your blog is the most important social media element your company can create. As such, it needs to be a part of your main website and it must support your brand. Just having a blog up somewhere on the World Wide Web doesn't cut it. In fact, you can have the most informational, well-organized blog in the world, but if it isn't an integrated part of your website, it's useless.

Unfortunately, many businesses have a blog that acts like its own website and is totally separate from the company's main website. As such, the blog often gets more traffic and better web rankings than the main site. The blog gets all the credit for the business owner's well thought-out, regular posts and the website gets none. *Ideally, you want your website to get everything.*

The goal is not for consumers to just read your blog; it's for them to read your blog and then visit your website and take action.

Therefore, port your blog directly into your main website. Ideally, users will see the same header and footer as the main website, making it very easy for them to jump from a blog post to a relevant section on your website.

Tip #2: A Little Keyword Research Goes a Long Way

If you are going to take the time and effort to keep your social media platforms up-to-date and informational, then you probably want your potential customers to read them. The true power of social media marketing is the ability to gain search engine ranking by optimizing your platforms, thereby getting found in the search engines and getting traffic to your platforms.

Chances are you've already done the hard work. You're giving great information, uploading videos and images, and giving customers a real value-add. Now you simply need to pick one strategic keyword per post and do a little post optimization, and you'll have search engine ranking. For each blog, use a keyword tool (such as Google's free one: *adwords.google.com/select/KeywordToolExternal*); find a keyword with good search volume, and simply add it into your post title and throughout the content.

Now, here is the trick for using a keyword tool to localize posts. You probably won't see the tools diving in deep enough to get search volume for Fairfield, Virginia, or any other town for that matter. However, what works for Americans, works for "Fairfieldians." This means if there is great search volume under "Cosmetic Dentistry," for example, then there is probably good search volume under "Cosmetic Dentistry, Fairfield VA." So think global, but act local with your keywords.

Get Local

When it comes to marketing on the Internet, the sky is truly the limit for really narrowing in and getting in front of your target audience. Local searching is no exception. Here are a few tricks of the trade that can help you dominate local search results.

Tip #1: Use *Geo-Targeting* Carefully

Many local businesses that do Pay Per Click advertising use geo-targeted criteria, which means your PPC ad will only show if the searcher has a local IP address in the geographic area you've defined. The biggest gap in only running a "geo-targeted by IP address" campaign is that people who are not physically located in your area when searching won't see your ads. So if someone lives around the corner from you, but happen to be across the country visiting their Aunt Betty and using her computer to find some local businesses to call next week when they're back in town, your PPC ads won't show.

For this reason, geo-targeted Pay Per Click accounts need to have two campaigns. Campaign 1 is the localized campaign that only shows ads to consumers in your area, and Campaign 2 is a state-wide or national campaign with keywords that have local modifiers.

Using our cosmetic dentistry above, in Campaign 1, you could show ads for keywords such as "cosmetic dentistry," knowing that only consumers in the surrounding areas would see them. For Campaign 2, you could show ads for keywords such as "cosmetic dentistry Fairfield VA," knowing that regardless of where that person is currently located, they have a need for a dentist in Fairfield.

Tip #2: Use Local Business Center Ads

Local Business Center ads are a fantastic way to gain additional, localized ranking in the search engines. Setting up a Local Business Center ad account in Google is free—all you need is a local address and you are good to go.

Local Business Center gives you the opportunity to connect your local listings with your Google Adwords account, meaning that when someone searches for your keyword in your local area, your listing will appear with an address and phone number under the standard ad text. Even better, Local Business Center ads can be optimized. For example, if one of your local listings is titled "Fairfield Dentist," you could label it "Fairfield Dentist, Cosmetic Dentistry" and gain ranking for someone searching for cosmetic dentistry in Fairfield.

By using a keyword tool and including your keyword in the local listing, small business can take full advantage of a local Internet Marketing approach.

Tip #3: Get the Right Local Domain for the Right Audience

As much as we are targeting local keywords and local listings, there is a fine line between local and too local. For example, some businesses put their phone number or address (or part of it) in their domain name. Whereas an address and/or phone number is certainly local, it is just a bit too local. Searchers definitely identify with localized keywords; however, typically they don't search down to the street-number or phone number level until they are looking for directions or a specific provider. It's better to get a website address that is local-keyword rich. A small change in your web address can make a very big change in your search engine Findability.

Dominate Your Local Market for Results!

Yes, you can dominate your local market. By utilizing the strategies covered, you can up your game on the local competitors. Ideally, you want to be the ONLY provider in town as far as the search engines are concerned. With so many people going online to get their local needs met, this is one area of your web marketing campaign you can't afford to overlook.

Rule of Thumb

Social media has changed how business reaches and communicates with its customers and potential customers. Still in its infancy, it will continue to evolve. With an effective social media campaign, businesses will find that their marketing dollars will be re-allocated.

D-Bar's Keegan Gerhard has already seen the benefit of marketing via Facebook.

You can go store to store for the most perfect, organic, handpicked produce in the whole wide world. You can run the most amazing specials all day long. But if people don't know you're doing it, and you don't want to spend money on advertising dollars— where does it get you? But it doesn't cost me anything to Tweet or post on Facebook about what I'm doing.

The best thing about posting what I'm doing online is that I get feedback. I have concrete evidence that people saw what I posted. We can offer something like a "family friendly rate." We can craft it however we want, and get concrete feedback on whether it worked or whether it didn't.

Still not convinced? We asked Keegan what words of encouragement he would give to CEO's, entrepreneurs and business owners about taking the plunge into social media marketing.

You cannot stereotype what social media is. Social media is not an elevated form of kid's texting. It's not just about what I did Friday night after I hung out with my girlfriend.

(continued)

Social media is a way to present yourself to the world very inexpensively, and it can be crafted exactly the way that you want it.

You're given the social media tools to craft your image the way you want, and share it with the world. How could you do that in the past without spending tens or hundreds of thousands of dollars? How could you possibly do that?

With Facebook, you can get exposure, tell the world who you really are, and create that all-important buzz. Marketers know that the "buzz factor" is one of the most important elements in creating buy-in. The Internet and savvy use of the five key social media platforms has created the fast track. Your customers are using it ... and so must you.

You just finished this chapter. Congratulations! Now tell us what you think, the tools you use and get additional offers and giveaways. Scan this QR Code with your smartphone or go to *Findability.com/Thumbonomics7* for more Facebook insights.

8

Twitter Findability

Twitter:
The Quick and Easy Way to Communicate

Is it really possible to say anything meaningful or useful in only 140 characters?
(82 characters)

Twenty percent of current Internet users would answer with a resounding "YES!"
(78 characters)

By 2011, 200+ million users embraced Twitter, the rapidly growing micro-blogging site that takes advantage of the popularity of texting.
(136 characters)

How important has Twitter become? Two significant events occurred within the first three months of 2011. Events that were thousands of miles apart, with limited reporting initially, yet the world following them closely. All because of Twitter postings from people on the inside.

With breaking events, it's common to see information going out via Twitter feeds. With the uprising in Egypt and earthquake/tsunami in Japan, those on the inside were able to stay connected with those on the outside because of the flow of tweets created. The world was hungry for information. Twitter was there when traditional media couldn't be.

Twitter is probably the least understood of the big five. According to *Twitter.com*,

> Twitter is a real-time information network powered by people all around the world, which lets you share and discover what's happening now. (138 characters)

Sound like something you could make use of?

I think of Twitter as the world's largest text chat session, or chat room. Everyone can join in, they can connect with people they respect; people they want to follow and learn more about.

On Twitter, you have short, 140 character conversations. The 140 character limit originated so tweets could be sent as mobile text messages (which have a limit of 160 characters). Subtract 20 characters for author signature and URL and it gives users just enough room.

Even if you personally find the whole idea of "tweeting" inane, you don't understand it at all, and think it would be a totally ineffective method of communication for your organization—please don't negate how other people choose to communicate. Don't cut off your nose to spite your face!

Comcast Tweets—and So Should YOU!

Bill Gerth, head of Comcast DMO Group

We interviewed the cable giant Comcast to understand how social media helped them enhance their reputation for great customer service and connect with their customers via Twitter. Here is what Comcast's Bill Gerth, also known as "Comcast Bill," has to say about their Twitter start up:

> We know that people have different preferences for how they like to communicate, and being in the social media space gives us a way to reach our customers who use that space.
>
> The Digital Media Outreach (DMO) Team was created in late 2007 with just three members and quickly grew to become a six-person team by 2008. Initially the team would go onto different social media sites, blogs and forums where people were talking about Comcast and ask the simple question, *"How can I help?"* Currently, the team is comprised of eight members and has expanded into many other social platforms where our customers are present and comfortable.

Notice that last line in particular—"where our customers are *present and comfortable.*"

People from teens and up are very, very comfortable with text messaging. As these younger generations start moving up in their careers and earning levels; as they're starting to buy more and more services and products—naturally they'll choose methods of getting information that they are most comfortable with. They probably will not read the local *PennySaver* or articles from the *Harvard Business Review.*

Comcast Bill discovered that Tweeting to their customers provides cutting edge information and customer service:

> …being in the social media space gives us a way to reach our customers who use that space. In addition, sites like Twitter give us a great real-time view into what's happening and what people are thinking. Providing customer service via social media is just one of the ways we're working to improve the customer experience, and it's really a win-win for our customers and for us.

Twitter is the faster, more condensed method of communication. It consists of a stream of quick and easy messages … perfect for communicating with busy people who want to stay connected, but are short on time.

Getting Real, Bottom Line Results from Twitter

Setting up a Twitter account is easy, and user friendly. Here's what you need to know:

1. **Set up a professional account name.** I have *Twitter.com/HeatherLutze*. Since I am the face of my brand, I started with my own name. I could have also gone with Twitter.com/Findability or *Twitter.com/FindabilityFormula* which would have been representative of my entire brand, not just me as a speaker and an author.

   You may want to reserve all your trademarks, brand names, product names or service space names as well as capture and reserve your company name. (It's OK to have more than one Twitter account.)

   You can either build Twitter accounts on each of those names or you can have one tweet that shows up on each account, which points people back to the primary brand. In other words, you can redirect all your Twitter accounts back to the primary, official company Twitter location. Why? So if someone searches for you under one of your product names, they will find you, and be directed back to your main Twitter account.

2. **Make your site as professional as possible.** For that reason, don't use the templates Twitter provides—they look extremely unprofessional, and generic. You don't want the same background as your customers or your nephew. Although the templates are fine for a personal account, they don't work for a business.

Elements to Include in Your Background Design

- Your logo
- Any call to action—meaning what you would like them to do as a result of visiting your Twitter account.
- Your contact information—phone number, email address, website address. This information needs to be an integral part of the visible area—it will be seen to the left and right hand sides of the "tweet stream."

  Hire a designer who knows how to do that correctly. There are many different screen resolutions available; a good designer will understand how to build a page that is readable on all of them.

3. **In the set-up process, you'll be asked to name your account and write a profile description.** What do you need to include in your profile description? Yes, you guessed it—**one or more important keyword phrases.**

An excellent website is *99designs.com*, *CrowdSpring.com* and *Fiverr.com.* They all have an arsenal of designers who will do a very professional background for you for minimal moneys.

4. **Decide who will become the face of your Twitter presence.** This is an important decision. Twitter users, and social media users in general, don't want to converse with a logo. They don't want to communicate with some kind of entity that's just the generic voice of the brand; they don't want to read tweets from the GEICO gecko. People want to follow people, even if they are dealing with corporate giants.

   If you look on the "Comcast Cares" site, there's always a picture of a person—whether it is actually Bill, or whoever's managing that account—there's his picture. All the tweets come from him, so you know who you are actually communicating with.

   If, on the other hand, you have a specific product that is the main component of your Twitter campaign, in that case it's OK to use a very specific campaign logo like Tide detergent does, with their, "Tide Loads of Hope" program.

Their Twitter account uses the Tide Cares logo instead of a person's photo, but all their tweets are extremely *informative and personable*.

If your company is not that specifically focused, it's highly recommended to use a picture of a person. That goes over much better, particularly with the business-to-business audience. Remember, the whole point is building relationships.

5. **Use a picture of a real person in your organization and identify them by name.** All your tweets should be coming from that person, written in the first person. Make sure that you put a personal, warm and engaging voice to your Twitter account.

Comcast's Bill Gerth tells us with his accompanying photo:

> I am the only Bill (*@ComcastBill*) on our team right now. Will (*@ComcastWill*) has a similar handle and is the newest member of our team who's doing a fantastic job on Twitter.

6. **Use a series of tweets to make an impact.** We recommend that you create different groupings of tweets.

Pick one keyword phrase for each series of tweets, and use it consistently in each one. I usually put the keyword at the front of the tweet.

For instance, "Findability tip" would be my keyword. Then I put a colon, then the tip, and then the shortened URL at the end of the tweet.

7. **Set up a tweeting plan covering the next 30 days.** I sat down with my team and put together a strategy for writing all the tweets for the coming month. If you do it this way, you can be very methodical about what you include in your tweets and what keywords you'll use with each grouping of tweets. It will be a cohesive, cleverly directed approach, instead of a hodgepodge of tweets off the top of someone's head.

No surprise—I want you to always include a keyword phrase in each tweet.

Tweet Style Suggestions

- **Quotes:** a great way to show people that you're really plugged in to your industry. Here at the Findability Group, we often quote Microsoft's founder Bill Gates and Matt Cutts from Google. We quote famous founders of companies. Anybody that is an industry visionary in our arena is likely to find a quote about them within our Twitter postings.

- **Industry facts and news buzz:** included any events that are happening, both internally and externally to your company. In ours, we include any speaking engagements that I may be doing.

- **Tools and applications:** people absolutely love new tools. When you tweet about tools, remember to include their URL so your followers can check them out for themselves.

- **Fun things:** such as jokes, witty cartoons, etc. These add liveliness and personality to your tweets.
- **Retweets (RT):** the name is self explanatory—you receive a "tweet" in your account and re-send it to everyone who follows you, all with a click that takes less than five seconds.

We use a tool called *SocialOomph.com*, which has "tweet alerts." You can enter keyword phrases, and get a roundup at the end of every day showing who used them. I can find out everyone who tweeted about my name, my company's name, or my book. Using my book as an example, I'll then retweet people's comments about the book, or people's comments about presentations we give, so everyone who follows me on Twitter will see them.

One caveat—before you ever retweet someone else's information, visit the URL. Make sure that you are willing to endorse the material attached to the tweet. You never want to embarrass yourself by mistakenly forwarding something inappropriate, or something you don't really believe in.

- **Promotional codes and coupons:** perfect on Twitter; they keep people engaged. You can use special promo codes and hash tags as part of your tweets. This is a great way to do some marketing— ask your followers certain questions, and then give them something in return.

Hashtags Create Instant Feedback

For many, hashtags are unfamiliar. Affiliated with Twitter accounts, you can create a unique word or short phrase that other Twitterers can hone in on quickly. Looking for what hashtag is being used in your industry or where the "buzz" is, go to *HashTags.org* and see the trending hashtags.

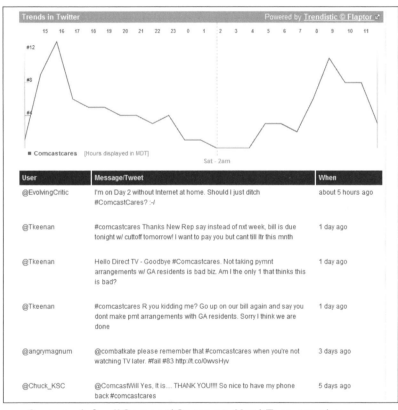

As search for #ComcastCares on *HashTags.org* shows us
in real time and historical tweets!
You can do this for your hashtag too. Cool.

I was speaking at the Online Marketing Summit (OMS) in San Diego and we tweeted, using the hashtag, *#getfound*. The # is the hash and then *getfound* is the tag that I associated with that speaking event.

By the end of the event, I had 50 plus tweets of everyone who had used *#getfound* during my session. People were quoting me and people talking about issues I'd brought up in the session. Comments were made about how I rocked; how I connected; how I was practical and my strategies and recommendations were immediately useable. My name, the title of my book, and those comments were circulated to everyone that was on the sender's list of followers. I got excellent, live feedback!

Word of mouth is so important—the hashtag I created at the one event was being read by everyone in the workshop, plus ALL their followers. That's a huge network.

If you have a particular phrasing for your products, or a phrase that is really comfortable for your business, you can use it to create that hashtag. For my company, it could be *#findability* or *#getfound*. For OMS it was *#OMSNY*. There is nothing to set up with a hashtag, just use it. Not once, but on a repeat basis.

From a findability standpoint, if you know there's already a hashtag out there for an event you're going to, or a conference you're going to, make sure to use that hashtag inside of your tweets.

You can have multiple hashtags in one tweet. The benefit is that it begins aggregating the conversation around what you're talking about as well, and includes you in the

groberts23 @HeatherLutze - Great presentation at #SESNY today! Very engaging. Wish you had more time!
Friday, 25 March 2011, 3:14 pm - Reply - View Tweet - Retweet - Direct Message

doncooper #FF Social media tips: @HeatherLutze @davidnour @SocialNetDaily @Ginaschreck @LinkedInDiva @copyblogger @MikeONeilDenver
Friday, 25 March 2011, 2:42 pm - Reply - View Tweet - Retweet - Direct Message

WorldOfLiquor @HeatherLutze Thanks for all the great information. Look forward to putting it in to practice!
Friday, 25 March 2011, 1:32 pm - Reply - View Tweet - Retweet - Direct Message

yasminbendror Great @HeatherLutze session at SES NY on how searchers FIND u on #socialmedia channels: think like a consumer, don't drink yr own cool-aid!
Friday, 25 March 2011, 12:25 pm - Reply - View Tweet - Retweet - Direct Message

beckydharris RT @OMSummit: Always Use Hashtags in your tweets, make sure they are key word optimized as well.#GetFound #OMSNY via @HeatherLutze
Friday, 25 March 2011, 12:09 pm - Reply - View Tweet - Retweet - Direct Message

Notice that I was able to get all tweets from @HeatherLutze and #Getfound as well as #OMSNY.

conversation for that particular event or conversation. It's a way to keep you in the buzz and expand your branding. To avoid looking like spam, limit the number of hashtags to less than three. Don't overload your tweets with them; it's not necessary to include a hashtag every time you tweet.

Ultimately, your social media brand manager would be responsible for setting up and automating these tweets. For a huge corporation like Comcast, they have an entire department. When asked if anyone within the Comcast organization could Tweet directly with their customers, Bill told us,

Our National Customer Operations group and the DMO Team are responsible for interacting directly with customers online, and this is really to help ensure we're providing consistent and up-to-date information in a timely way. We also receive ongoing training and have access to different internal systems and programs, like our GrandSlam troubleshooting portal, so we can help customers.

Twitter Etiquette—the "Don'ts"

There are many *faux pas* people make in the process of tweeting that can have undesired consequences. I'm just going to tell you my "top ten" pet peeves in regard to tweets. (Actually, there are eleven …)

This might seem like a long list, but most of them are just common courtesy, and common sense.

1. **Avoid tweeting too often.** Don't drown your "tweet stream" with too much information. Too many tweets will overwhelm people, and cause them to *unfriend* you or *unfollow* you. Instead, spread out your tweets over time.

2. **Limit your retweeting—and do not retweet yourself.** If someone retweets a quote or something that you said, you can retweet it, if it seems important—just do it prudently. Retweeting things you've already tweeted comes across as narcissistic. Many people become very uncomfortable with that, and will drop you. When someone retweets you, it's common to send

them a direct message (DM) saying thank you—
you do this by putting the @ sign in front of their
twitter name, or click on "send direct message"
when in Twitter like this:

HeatherLutze
Thanks for the follow! Let's stay connected! If you're
looking for search marketing tips, check out this great
resource- http://goo.gl/Vz5HI
31 Jan at 23:35

3. **Don't hard sell your product or service** in your
   tweets. That's not what Twitter is about, and it's
   the fastest way to turn people off.
4. **Don't rely on promo codes or coupons** in your
   tweet stream. Make sure to really mix it up, using
   a nice, wide variety of tweets with different styles
   and approaches, throughout the day and the
   month.
5. **Avoid spamming.** Be mindful that people
   following you on Twitter really want to get viable
   information about your company and what you
   do. Make sure that you're not spamming just to
   try and get people onto your website. You can be
   thrown off Twitter entirely for spamming, so be
   careful about that.
6. **Don't tweet if you've been drinking,** known as
   "twunking." Believe it or not, I've seen it with
   some of my past clients. They have a big party or

happy hour, and everyone is merrily tweeting away with reckless abandon! The tweets that come out of that can be very embarrassing. (Use your imagination …) Obviously, use discernment and be mindful of when to tweet and when not to tweet.

7. **Never say anything on Twitter you wouldn't want known as common knowledge about your company.** Know that if you put it out there, it will spread like wildfire. There are no "takebacks" with tweets or anything else that goes out over the internet. Be thoughtful about what you share and how you share it.

8. **Tweeting too little is as problematic as tweeting too much.** If you only tweet once a month, people following you won't regard you as a credible expert. Start off on the low side, perhaps two to three tweets **a day** in the beginning; moving up to **four to five tweets per day** when you become used to it, and confident about your strategy. Make sure they're not all the same style of tweets, that there are a variety of tweets to keep people interested and engaged.

9. **Never pretend to be someone else.** Always be authentic and represent yourself in first person. Don't talk about yourself in the third person.

10. **Don't tweet what you had for lunch,** the weather, that you're bored, or that you have nothing to tweet about. Keep it extremely professional and

business related. You can let your personality show and have a little bit of fun, but always keep it professional by using professional language. Don't use four letter words or purposely say anything inflammatory. Keep it totally above board.

11. **Never tweet when you're upset.** You'll probably cringe over what you wrote later, after you've calmed down.

    However … Even though I'm telling you not to do it, I have to admit I did just that when I was really upset with an airline on my personal Twitter account. This is one of the areas in which Twitter shines. As a consumer, you can tweet that you're frustrated with a company, and see if you get a response from them. Businesses are watching what's said about them, and you should be watching what's said about your firm as well.

    One of my favorite books is *Twitter Power* by Joel Comm. This excellent book has wonderful case studies about companies that are hyper-vigilant about watching tweets and responding to them. They are protecting and enhancing their brand in real-time, one of the most powerful things about Twitter.

You might be amazed at how quickly a tweeted complaint gets a response, especially from big firms like @Southwest Airlines (#SouthWestAir) and @Delta (#Delta).

> It's simply good corporate policy to commit to watching tweets about your organization and quickly respond to them.

When we asked Bill about his personal experience with customers via Twitter, he was pretty enthusiastic:

> I can say that every interaction I have had with a customer has a put a smile on my face—either because it was funny or because I was able to help them.
>
> For me, knowing that I made a marked difference for an individual customer who may now think better of Comcast and our customer support is what drives my passion for my job. A customer response that shows appreciation or an unexpected delight … these are the things that I cherish.

Are you starting to see the possibilities of Twitter for your organization?

Your Twitter Action Plan

1. **Set up your accounts,** each one with custom backgrounds. Make sure each separate account you own on Twitter has at least one tweet welcoming people to your space.

2. **Create keyword rich profiles,** full of relevant content.

3. **Have your 30 day tweet plan ready to go** before you activate your Twitter account. Get your social media team into high gear. They will write out all tweets for the coming month, keeping in mind the recommendations I've given for tweeting variety.

4. **Automate your tweets,** so you can all get back to work. No one should have to hand feed tweets all day long. This doesn't mean to ignore them; you need to respond to relevant postings and monitor what others are saying. Choose to engage. Use a program, such as *Hootsuite.com* or *TweetDeck.com*, to make your social media strategies manageable.

And last, but not least ...

5. **Start building followers.** This is the biggie—without followers reading your tweets, you are just spinning your wheels. The more followers you have, the more your name, and your brand is out there—which is what your social media platform is designed to do.

You will build followers by doing the following:

- Invite everyone inside your company to follow you.

- Provide great content in your tweets.
- You must also be a follower to build followers. Follow industry leaders. For instance, you can follow Apple's Steve Jobs, or someone who is an industry leader in your own arena—and then follow his/her followers.
- When you follow "followers" of others, it's common for them to follow you in return. Why? Because they've already indicated that they have an interest in your field—you did so by following someone already there.
- On your website, Facebook and LinkedIn pages, display the icon for Twitter with a "follow" suggestion. When a visitor clicks on it, he is taken to your account where he clicks again to verify he wants to follow you. This takes less than five seconds.
- Include Twitter, Facebook, YouTube and LinkedIn addresses on your business card and other promotional material.
- Do a special announcement to your existing email contacts that you can be followed on Twitter, Facebook, YouTube and LinkedIn.
- On your email signature, include a "Follow me or us" on Twitter, Facebook, YouTube and LinkedIn with addresses for each that are live links—a click away and they become your followers.

Approach this carefully; don't start following thousands at a time. (That could put your account in jeopardy.) Visit every single profile of someone you're considering following. Does their account look legitimate? Do they have a custom background? Is there a real person's face? Is their profile description set up? What's the quality of their tweets?

Make sure that the people you're following are real tweeters; not spammers, or affiliate marketers.

Findability Makeover
"Fripped" Out Your Twitter ... Now What?
Twitter.com/Pfripp

I have Twitter, "now what?" I am hearing this more and more from clients every day. They have jumped on the social media band wagon, but now they have no idea what they should they be expecting from their efforts?

Patricia Fripp, a well known speaker and executive speech coach, is asking herself the same question. In March of 2009, Patricia decided to join the Twitter community, and she has grown her "followers" from a non-existent account to over *3,763* members in just one year. She is diligently Tweeting and doing everything right from a "Findability inside of Twitter" standpoint. If you search using *search.twitter.com* you will see her using her main keyword "executive speech coach" in her tweets.

But what now? Why is she putting all this effort in? How does she capitalize on Twitter for business results? In her words:

I have bursts of enthusiasm about social media …
I assume key word rich tweets are not going to
hurt, but I am not aware of any booked business
from Twitter.

This Findability Makeover is about taking your efforts
to the next step. You cannot just throw yourself into social
media without understanding your end game. Whether it
is real business, sales leads, networking or just fun, as a
business, Patricia started aggressively tweeting and pushing information on to her tweet stream but did not think
about her overall objective.

Objective

Get more clients from Twitter by driving more traffic to her
main website, *Fripp.com*, and incentivizing them with articles
and giveaways. Hook them in and keep them hungry for her
Patricia Fripp Insights.

Problem

Patricia Fripp has a huge, growing following with lackluster
business results. How does she turn this following community into new clients?

Twitter Action Plan

- Check The Fundamentals First
- Analyze & Make It Better
- Continue using Keywords in your tweets for
  Findability

Check the Fundamental Elements
of Your Twitter Account

Before we look ahead, we must make sure we have a solid foundation. Check these fundamental elements of your Twitter account first.

Professional Looking Background

Patricia's background was great a year ago, but I would recommend she update this with a call to action and a clear outcome of working with her, as well as prominent phone number and website address. Think of your Twitter profile-page as a mini-website—a professional look with calls to action are very important. Also, testing different looks and feels are great in this forum.

1. **Time Management Tools (A Must!):** Setup a tool for monitoring and conversation management. I recommend a few free tools— *Ping.fm, SocialOomph, Hootsuite.* Remember, taking an hour to program in 30 Tweets for next month can save you hours of social media updating in the future.

2. **Setup a Measurement System:** Your measurement system will completely depend on the goals you have associated with your Twitter account. In Patricia's instance, her goal is to drive traffic to her website, then convert them to a lead. For this type of measurement,

Google Analytics is your best tool. In addition to setting up tracking codes for each link, you can measure very extensive amounts of data with this tool. For example, in Patricia's case, she has had:

- 257 visits to her website from Twitter;
- Average time on her site from Twitter visitors 1 minute, 26 seconds;
- Average visitor visits at least 2 pages; and
- 60 percent of visitors are unique visitors, never been to her site before.

Of course, one of the pieces of information missing in this data is conversions—how many people who visited Patricia's website "took action" (such as, a form-fill or a shopping cart purchase). By tracking conversions, Patricia will be able to start measuring what Tweet posts were more likely to drive traffic to the website that then converted to another action.

3. **Tweet Twice a Day—Testing Calls to Action, Keywords and Links:** Every Twitter follower wants different information. It's very important to try lots of different Twitter tactics (calls to action, keywords, links, etc.) to determine what your target audience wants the most.

Analyze & Make It Better

Ninety Nine percent of my tweets are giving advice in my areas of expertise … I enjoy seeing my quotes being retweeted.

—Patricia Fripp

Now that Patricia has been tweeting for awhile, it's time to start analyzing what Tweet posts are more successful. Patricia has stated her main objective for Twitter is to get leads, yet her self-identified "success" metric with Twitter seems to be re-tweets. A big reason Patricia's enthusiasm may wane with Twitter is she is optimizing her Tweets for re-Tweets, when instead she should be optimizing them based on bottom-line results.

Before analyzing an account, it's important to determine the metrics that demonstrate success of the business goal you have established. In this instance, we are measuring the traffic received from *Twitter.com* to *Fripp.com*, as tracked by Google Analytics, instead of re-tweets.

With Patricia, the end goal is not to get a "retweet" but instead to get Twitter traffic to the website to learn more about her services. As such, we are measuring the Tweets that included a link to the *Fripp.com* website, to determine how successful they were in driving traffic to the main website. This will give us great insight into how to optimize the account for better business results.

Measure for Results, NOT Traffic:
Use Productivity Tool More Effectively

If you want to measure the clicks to all links you give in tweets, not just website traffic, a good additional tool to implement is *HootSuite.com*. Hootsuite will measure the number of clicks you receive. However, it is important to note that HootSuite only measures clicks, whereas Google Analytics can measure a great deal more, pages/visit, unique visitors, and if they converted to a sale/lead. Google Analytics, however, is limited in the fact that it can only measure the traffic to your website—it can't measure the traffic you send to other websites from Twitter.

Analyze Past Tweets & Take Your Tweeting
to the Next Level

Let's take a look at the most successful Tweets in the account (based on the website traffic they sent to *Fripp.com*).

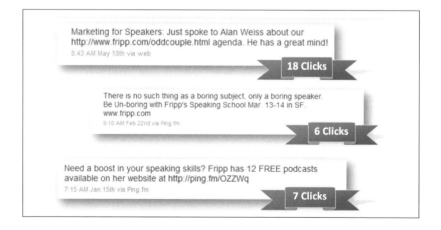

Successful elements to continue incorporating:

1. **Include Links as Much as Possible:** Whatever tracking you have setup (HootSuite or Google Analytics); the best way to track your success is by measuring the next step that people take. It's nice that people join your community, but what's valuable is in them taking the next step and visiting your website and eventually converting to a lead or sale. Consider a Twitter landing page welcoming them and a special offer for your loyal followers.

2. **Keywords:** "Marketing for Speakers" and "Speaking Skills" and "Speaking School" seem to be very effective Twitter keywords. We'd recommend using them more.

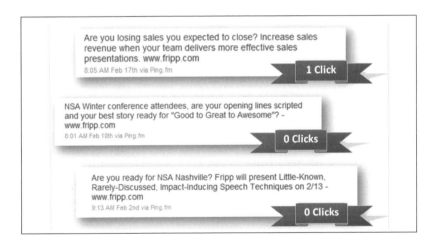

3. **NSA Specific Tweets**: These aren't as successful, which shows that we still need to test NSA keywords to find something they can find.

   > *Recommendation*: if you are tweeting for a specific event, like "National Speakers Association Winter Conference," see if they have setup a hashtag for the event. Likely, Patricia didn't get as much traffic because twitter-savvy event attendees knew to look for that hashtag (#NSA).

4. **Don't Be Too Sale-zy:** Try softer sales, a bit more calls to action & maybe giving something for free. 12 free podcasts is a lot more compelling to this audience then a direct speaking pitch.

Findability is about being present when the community searches for you, but it also means giving them a valuable interaction once they click. Tracking and market intelligence can go a long way in delivering your target audience the information they find meaningful in your Twitter account. Being able to really connect meaningfully with your audience by producing targeted, well-thought-out posts is the ideal way to optimize your Twitter account to not only bring you followers, but bring you leads.

Rule of Thumb

Initially, this will be time consuming. The work can be delegated amongst the various members of your social media committee. Trust me, it will be worth it!

Twitter is a perfect portal for businesses. On their site, they offer tips and case studies from businesses that have effectively used Twitter to build their brand and connect more personally with their customers. Check out:

business.twitter.com/twitter101/

You just finished this chapter. Congratulations! Now tell us what you think, the tools you use, and get additional offers and giveaways. Scan this QR Code with your smartphone or go to *Findability.com/Thumbonomics8* for more Twitter insights. You will also have access to the full Audio and PDF download of the FULL INTERVIEW with Bill Gerth of Comcast DMO Team. Enjoy!

9

LinkedIn Findability

In the Business Marketing Race?
LinkedIn's Your Marketing Place!

Although it might not get the same amount of press as Facebook or Twitter, LinkedIn is no lightweight in terms of business marketing potential. Executives from all the Fortune 500 companies have accounts on this B2B portal. In fact, business connections are the purpose of this site, giving it quite a different flavor than any of the others.

A Decision-Making Clientele

LinkedIn currently has about sixty-five million members, in over 200 countries worldwide. Their average age is 41—and get this—the average household income on LinkedIn is $109,000 per year!

Forty-nine percent of all LinkedIn members are business decision makers. You know when you use this site you're marketing to a highly targeted purchasing audience.

LinkedIn can be useful in different ways than the other social media portals ...

While writing *The Findability Formula*, I used LinkedIn extensively to source other search marketing professionals as well as other business owners, asking questions such as:

- What are your frustrations with search marketing and findability?
- What have been the worst experiences you've had with search marketing companies?

Their feedback provided a lot of the direction for *The Findability Formula*. I easily collected information, recommendations and testimonials from clients who had hired me as a speaker or used my consulting services. The result:

Real recommendations and testimonials from other professionals in my field. I have asked thousands of people at speaking engagements, "What's the first thing that goes through your head when you read a testimonial? I always get, "Their Mother wrote it?" or, "I feel like they made it up."

Why, then, do we keep putting testimonials on our websites? The answer is usually:

It's what our competitor is doing, or no one gave us a better option.

LinkedIn is a much more powerful "testimonial" or "referral" source. After speaking to dozens of CEO groups with Vistage International over the last two years, without questions, CEOs polled about whether they use and source services in LinkedIn, 99 percent answered YES. I reached out to my LinkedIn friends and asked them how they used LinkedIn for business. Here are some of their responses:

 Ellen Saravis Linkedin is an excellent portal to learn about other ☒ companies and what they are up to, and introduce myself & my company & see what kind of collaboration we can have together & how I can be of service to them! BTW, love your articles in Website mag!
about an hour ago · Unlike · 👍 1 person

 Susan Hyatt I know there is so much more I could do. I mainly use LinkedIn to get updates on where people I have worked with over time are these days with an eye to seeing if there may be some new point of professional connection that I should explore. Also, I use it to get the latest in news updates about corporate philanthropy.
about an hour ago · Unlike · 👍 1 person

 Bob Tipton Linked In's value to me is ALL about the groups to which I belong. They provide a way to narrow the massive opportunities and breadth of network reach offered by Linked In into manageable, bit-sized pieces. I call them my "Linked In on a Bun" (sounds like a new book title!)
about an hour ago · Like · 👍 2 people

 Robert Stack Heather don't know if get this in time. I am known as the FAME COACH (work with celebrity experts, best-selling authors, and international speakers). I use to take Linkedin for granted and never really paid attention to its value or who was following me. Then recently I was working on a national project for a major charity I support and I realized that Linkedin was a great resource for potential sponsors and way to directly connect with executives. I started reviewing my contacts and the more I reviewed those following me the more I realized I had accumulated a gold mine of contacts. My advice is for people to take a look at who is following you. My bet is they are probably probably sitting on a rather significant list of potential clients, sponsors, alliances, joint venture partners, and don't even realize that all they have to do is take time to see whose in your network. Open your eyes and the "contacts" will appear. That my tidbit for you Heather.
20 minutes ago · Unlike · 👍 2 people

 Corey Perlman Get introduced feature. Hands down the best, and most underutilized, feature on Linkedin.
24 seconds ago · Like

Other Great Uses for LinkedIn include:

- Use LinkedIn to represent your brand and your company as a strong, reliable entity. Enhance your credibility by showcasing professional connections and affiliations with other leaders in your field. One of the many strengths of this portal is that really powerful connections can be made.
- Check out the "Follow Company" feature. This allows you to keep up on developments within the companies you choose to follow, by sending you updates through your LinkedIn account.
- You can actually follow your competitors or key companies in your industry …
- You can follow visionaries you admire …
- You can follow trade journals or press and news related organizations …

    This feature is fantastic for doing some competitive intelligence work right inside of LinkedIn. No, there's nothing dishonest or sneaky about this: companies are only posting things they want to be publicly known anyway. It's simply a terrific way to keep abreast of news within your field.

Are you convinced that LinkedIn is for you? You should be!

The Set Up

To get the most of your LinkedIn account, let's start with the **set up.**

I want to show you how to use LinkedIn to provide your organization with a major marketing opportunity. Although not as big as Facebook, LinkedIn is spidered by search engines, and certainly does get ranked. *Spidering is when a search engine visits your website, grabs all the content and images and indexes them into its search engine.* Every employee has an optimized LinkedIn profile and it ranks under a high value keyword phrase in Google search results for your company. This is real, actionable visibility and Findability for your company. When each employee in your organization has their own LinkedIn profile, your organization is magnified on search engines because of your employees' connection to you. (These will all link to the main company profile.)

Here's the secret:

Each employee's profile will be optimized for a *different high value keyword phrase.* If you have 200 employees, this strategy provides you with 200 potential keyword-ranking opportunities!

(For an extra advantage—if someone is researching your firm, trying to decide if they want to do business with you— they will easily see you have X number of employees, all actively supporting and professionally representing your company.)

Are you getting a sense of the possibilities?

You already know your important keyword phrases. We talked about keyword research earlier in Chapter 5. *Social Media Marketing Keywords for Findability*. It's time to let that research pay off, in a big way.

Have your social media business manager assign one of these keyword phrases to each employee profile. I recommend a company-wide training, to show everyone how to optimize their profile for their particular keyword phrase.

Each employee will set up his/her own profile, based on that training. You need a hard deadline for your employees to finish their profiles, to be approved by the brand manager. Hopefully, as suggested in Chapter 4, *The Rules of Engagement*, your employees have already signed a social media document specifying what they can and cannot post on their profile.

It might make sense to start with only your social media committee creating LinkedIn accounts. Then add the rest of the company at some later date, when you have the whole routine down pat, and see how it's working for you.

Make sure to set up your official company profile before the employees set up individual ones. On LinkedIn's home page, click the word "more" at the top of the page, and then click on "companies." You'll see "add a company" on the right hand side of that page.

Once the employee profiles are approved, then they need to be linked with the company profile. For this purpose, each employee needs an email address at your company, such as: *John@MyCompany.com*.

Check out my profile and see how we have applied the method below:

Scan this link to see Heather's LinkedIn profile or go to *http://www. Linkedin.com/in/marketingspeakerHeatherLutze*

Tips for "Tricking Out" Your Profile

1. When each person sets up their personal profile, they will add a keyword to their last name. Using myself as an example, my name is entered as Heather Lutze-Internet Marketing Speaker. Use whatever high value keyword is most appropriate for that particular profile.

2. Make sure to also put a relevant keyword in the job description box. I wouldn't use corporate trainer or speaker as my job description; it's not specific enough. I would be an "Internet marketing Expert" or "Search Marketing Expert." That's the title of my position, and it includes the desired keywords.

3. Use the "additional information section" during the set up of all profiles. Add in all website addresses. For each website, there is a drop-down box, allowing you to indicate if the URL being added is a personal website, a company website, a blog, etc. The last selection is "other." Select the word "other" and a box will open allowing you to add a keyword-rich description of your site.

Instead of just putting *YourCompanyName.com*, you'll say, "Internet marketing speaker site." In the next box, you'll insert the company website's URL.

You can do several of these boxes, using different keyword phrases. I actually have *Internet marketing speaker site*, *Internet marketing consulting site* and *Internet marketing blog site*. It helps Google to optimize its search results when it sees these keywords with the link leading to their respective websites.

4. Of course, you are going to use your keyword phrase throughout the profile, including your summary, your specialties, your interests, your groups and associations, your honors and awards. Wherever it makes sense to include a keyword, make sure to do so.

5. Go to "Change public profile" under your settings tab. You'll see a space allowing you to customize your LinkedIn URL and include a keyword. Mine is *http://www.LinkedIn.com/in/MarketingSpeaker HeatherLutze*. (Notice I used no spaces between words.) This customized URL now provides yet another keyword indicator to Google of where to put my LinkedIn profile.

Sound complicated? I assure you it's not. Each of these big five portals has become popular partly because of what they have to offer, and partly because of their ease of use.

It's time to start linking all of your different social media efforts together...

Applications in LinkedIn

Under the "more" tab at the top of the page, you will find the "applications directory." According to LinkedIn,

> Applications enable you to enrich your profile, share and collaborate with your network, and get the key insights that help you be more effective.

There are different applications which allow your team to show blog posts and tweets, any company specific events, and many other things right on their LinkedIn homepage. It will be obvious to anyone who sees it that your company is pulling together in a very dedicated and professional way; that your employees are really "in the know."

In a word—*impressive.*

The beauty of applications is that once the profiles are completed and the applications added, no one has to touch their LinkedIn account again. And yet, the profiles will look extremely targeted, current and relevant.

The LinkedIn Action Plan

1. **Select keywords** for each of your social media committee profiles. (Or all employee profiles if you decide to open it up to the entire company.)
2. **Conduct a LinkedIn training** to show everyone how to optimize their own profile using their keyword phrase.

3. **Decide upon a firm deadline** for when those profiles need to be completed, and approved by the brand manager.
4. **Set up the official LinkedIn company profile** before activating the employee profiles, so they can be linked together.
5. **Add in the appropriate applications.**

I recommend starting with the social media team first, then moving on to your core executive teams and finally the entire company.

Every single employee's LinkedIn account should be evangelizing for your company, and showing all the other things you are doing as well. You want their profile to represent the individual employee—and also rank on any Google search.

If I see one of your employees' profiles showing up on Google and I click on it—I should see a hyper-relevant, current LinkedIn page; one that is clearly associated with your main company profile. You want to be on the cutting edge in every way people choose to connect with you.

Findability Makeover
LinkedIn Findability

LinkedIn has probably been the most useful tool I've implemented in my business practice and my book writing process. When I was writing my first book, *The Findability Formula*, LinkedIn was invaluable for sourcing other industry search marketing professionals. It was an easy and effective tool to connect with other thought leaders in the search marketing arena and check my work against how our agency runs.

What I never expected was that we could optimize our LinkedIn profiles to get found in search engine results. I believe most fellow business owners can agree with me on this point—if I am going to invest in using social media marketing, ideally, I want all my efforts to extend beyond the walls of the social media site to a much bigger findable audience that is interested in our products or services.

My team started looking at ways to tweak our clients' profiles, as well as our own, to rank for specific, long tail keywords; consequently, the profiles showed up in the search results. This started us on our path of testing Social Media Sites for search engine Findability, and to our delight it worked. Below is the strategy we discovered on how to optimize and maximize your profile for optimal Findability inside of LinkedIn, as well as getting your profile to rank in search engines.

Problem: *Sites like LinkedIn are not getting the leads, contacts and resources I expected. How can I leverage my time and effort in LinkedIn to get real business results?*

LinkedIn Findability Action Plan

- Choose Your Keywords.
- Optimize Key Elements in Your Profile.
- Use Applications to Enhance the Quality of Your Profile.
- Track Meaningful Results.

Choose Your Keywords

Most likely, you know the keywords you want to be found under. If not, use a keyword tool like *Google External Keyword Tool* and start looking for "shopping" keywords. By shopping, I mean that they are warm and semi-qualified, based on the keyword the searcher used.

Obviously, if you are Madonna or Bill Gates, you don't have to worry about people finding you. However, the rest of us have to work a bit harder to increase our "celebrity" in LinkedIn. Pick a keyword that is going to position you as a thought leader and an expert in your field—for example, my keyword is "Internet Marketing Speaker."

Optimize Key Elements in Your Profile

Here are the main elements for optimizing your LinkedIn Profile:

Element 1: Use a professional headshot in your profile; people connect with faces, not logos or a blank shadow of a person.

Element 2: Think of your name as your headline— it must have a keyword included. For your name field, keep your first name as is, for example mine is "Heather," however, in your last name field, include a keyword such as, "Lutze—Internet Marketing Speaker." Now you are findable under your name and your expertise.

Element 3: Keyword optimization techniques apply to LinkedIn as much as they apply to a page on your website. Make sure to include keywords throughout your profile, including specialties, job descriptions in the summary, etc., while using the same keyword phrase you selected in your name headline. See if you can bake in keywords without looking "spammy." Please remember, it's about spreading your phrases over your entire profile, NOT cramming in as many keywords as you can fit.

Element 4: Make sure to leverage your key website assets in the "sites" area. Use the drop down tab for the "sites" and select "other." This will allow you to put in your own keyword like "Internet Marketing Blog" to match your URL. You have *three* keywords you can leverage. Your keyword now functions as an anchor text and links to one of your assets, such as your blog, twitter profile or your website.

Element 5: Go after recommendations. When you are reaching out to colleagues, ask them to use specific keyword phrases or specific websites when they talk about your services. Make sure to actively give recommendations to people you have something great to comment about.

Below is my LinkedIn profile at the time of publication of *Thumbonomics*:

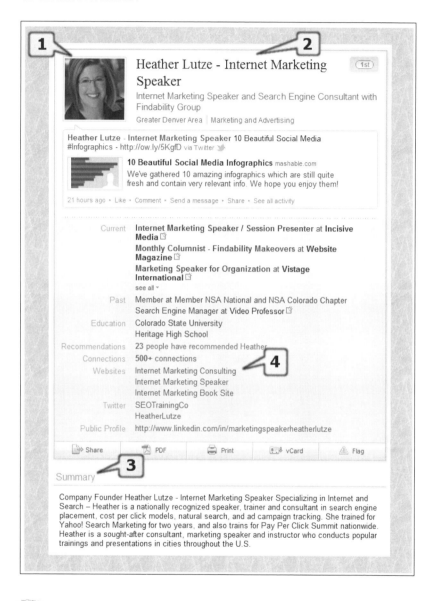

Heather Lutze - Internet Marketing Speaker (1st)

Internet Marketing Speaker and Search Engine Consultant with Findability Group

Greater Denver Area | Marketing and Advertising

Heather Lutze - Internet Marketing Speaker 10 Beautiful Social Media #Infographics - http://ow.ly/5KgfD via Twitter

10 Beautiful Social Media Infographics mashable.com
We've gathered 10 amazing infographics which are still quite fresh and contain very relevant info. We hope you enjoy them!

21 hours ago · Like · Comment · Send a message · Share · See all activity

Current	**Internet Marketing Speaker / Session Presenter** at **Incisive Media**
	Monthly Columnist - Findability Makeovers at **Website Magazine**
	Marketing Speaker for Organization at **Vistage International**
	see all ⌄
Past	Member at Member NSA National and NSA Colorado Chapter
	Search Engine Manager at Video Professor
Education	Colorado State University
	Heritage High School
Recommendations	23 people have recommended Heather
Connections	500+ connections
Websites	Internet Marketing Consulting
	Internet Marketing Speaker
	Internet Marketing Book Site
Twitter	SEOTrainingCo
	HeatherLutze
Public Profile	http://www.linkedin.com/in/marketingspeakerheatherlutze

Share | PDF | Print | vCard | Flag

Summary

Company Founder Heather Lutze - Internet Marketing Speaker Specializing in Internet and Search – Heather is a nationally recognized speaker, trainer and consultant in search engine placement, cost per click models, natural search, and ad campaign tracking. She trained for Yahoo! Search Marketing for two years, and also trains for Pay Per Click Summit nationwide. Heather is a sought-after consultant, marketing speaker and instructor who conducts popular trainings and presentations in cities throughout the U.S.

Use Applications to Enhance the Quality of Your Profile

LinkedIn applications are an easy way to maximize and automate your social media efforts on LinkedIn. You can use applications to pull your blog, tweet stream, as well as your favorite books and dynamically show them on your profile. This keeps your profile fresh, interesting and full of "thought leader" information that features you as an expert in your field. The great part is that you don't have to update it every time you update your blog or add a tweet; it will dynamically be fed from your blog or twitter account. You can even use this automation to dynamically update your status as well. Nice!

Track Meaningful Results

How do you know this optimization is really working? Here are a few Key Performance Indicators (KPIs) you can look for:

1. When you type in your keyword phrase from your optimized profile, does your profile show up?
2. Is your profile at 100 percent connectivity by the LinkedIn Rating Scale? Keep working toward the full amount and surpass it.
3. Are you getting an increase in recommendations? As you build your notoriety and keep connecting with colleagues, clients and associates, gifts will show up in the form of unsolicited recommendations. It really does make your day to receive one of these in your inbox.

4. You should see a steady increase of personal messages show up in your Inbox inside of LinkedIn. The more conversations you create and receive in LinkedIn, the more comfortable you will be using LinkedIn and building your community.
5. Watch for your profile in the search engines. If you choose the right keyword that is not too highly competitive, you will show up fast.

Some Thought Leaders to Follow on LinkedIn

There are a few LinkedIn profiles of professionals in my network that really shine. Here is a list of who I recommend you look up and follow what they are doing:

David Nour: *LinkedIn.com/in/davidnour*

Laura Stack: *LinkedIn.com/in/laurastack*

Gina Schreck: *LinkedIn.com/in/ginaschreck*

John Sileo: *LinkedIn.com/in/identitytheftspeaker*

Myself: *LinkedIn.com/in/marketingspeakerheatherlutze*

Feel free to find me on LinkedIn and copy how I have optimized my profile. Keep pushing the opportunity that social media marketing can provide. Keep in mind that these sites are search engines in themselves.

Findability is not a convention that is only held by search engines; portals like LinkedIn, Twitter and Facebook are search engines in their own right.

Rule of Thumb

I have personally found LinkedIn to be an amazing resource:

- for powerful business to business connections;
- for identifying new prospects and new opportunities;
- for keeping up with your industry leaders; and
- for ranking in Google under high value keywords for your company.

You just finished this chapter. Congratulations! Now tell us what you think, the tools you use, and get additional offers and giveaways. Scan this QR Code with your smartphone or go to *Findability.com/Thumbonomics9* for more LinkedIn insights.

10

YouTube Findability

Beat the Competition with
Your Own Marketing Video Channel

Every minute, 24 hours worth of brand new video content is uploaded to YouTube. Yes, every minute!

Who's watching?

Let's look at the numbers—48 percent of all Internet users have been to a video sharing site; out of those, 51 percent visit YouTube weekly or *more often*. These numbers will increase month by month after this book is published!

People have very individual tastes in how they like to learn or receive information. Receiving content via engaging customer videos is tremendously appealing to huge numbers of people. (For some—seeing is believing.)

Google is vigilant about not including specific graphics on search result pages, but YouTube videos really stand out. Not only do they quickly catch your eye on the search page, they're also keyword rich.

Keywords can and should be included in the title of a video, which will help it rank even faster. YouTube is an amazing tool for posting well targeted videos that are not just findable within YouTube, but also findable in the big search engine results.

Set Up Your Own Video Channel

To get started with YouTube, you'll set up a company YouTube channel. The name you choose is important—it needs to incorporate an important keyword phrase. If you have a graphic design company called "Go Creative," logically that is what you would call your channel. Instead of doing that, I want you to take advantage of an opportunity to provide more information, use one of your major keywords, and become more findable—by setting up your channel name as "Go Creative Graphic Design Denver."

After creating the actual name of the account, you'll be asked to create a profile. I know at this point, I don't even need to mention that this profile is for your business persona. (But, if you are skipping around, and not reading from start to finish, it's a point that must be made here.) This is not a personal page for your favorite YouTube videos. Everything you put into the profile needs to represent your company in a business-like manner. Be mindful of using keywords in the setup and throughout the profile. Preview mine at *YouTube.com/hlutze*.

It's All About the Video

Although I keep stressing keywords, equally important is artistic quality. At my company we use Kodak Zi8 high-definition video cameras, very similar to a flip camera. We take it to various events and quickly shoot and upload a new YouTube video; one that we've just taken on the spot, no editing required. Depending on which smartphone you have, you can actually stream video directly to YouTube.

I'm not talking about a Martin Scorsese production, rather something spontaneous we can upload just as it is. It usually has no front credits, no fancy music, and no scrolling credits at the back. We're looking for a genuine, authentic moment captured in these videos. Why? Because frequently, people feel that overproduced videos lack credibility.

I know I've angered several video production people with that point of view. After all, it's their livelihood to do fancy front work and precise editing throughout the video. But, oftentimes an overly produced, slick video is perceived as a hard sell. It's seen as an advertisement. What you need to remember about videos is their fans are most often watching for entertainment; they don't want to be sold.

For you, it's a good thing, because you don't need to hire a videographer or production team. These are videos anyone can get the hang of doing. In fact, that's the beauty of YouTube—it's for everyone—not just to watch, but to participate in. Go for that "reality show" style of video, where it's a little jerky and looks like you just walked into an interesting moment and captured it live. You'll find this style much more intriguing and credible for the YouTube audience than a well rehearsed and well edited piece of video.

What about the actual video content? Many corporations seem to struggle with this aspect. They are only used to slick, expensive, mega-produced employee manual videos, or annual report videos, complete with all kinds of special effects.

That's not what we are looking for with a YouTube marketing effort. Think of the difference between hip—and corporate. The question becomes, how do you strike a balance between producing something that is relevant to a searching audience on YouTube or on Google, but also that represents your brand with professionalism? This can be a bit tricky.

Keegan Gerhard of D Bar Desserts and Food Network

The D Bar Dessert Experience

It's no secret that I have a sweet tooth. Working with D Bar Desserts became a personal favorite—after all, how could I resist something that had a theme, "Changing the world one slice of cake at a time"? The star chef of the D Bar restaurant is Keegan Gerhard. You might know him from the Food Network Challenge.

When I first met Keegan to brainstorm social media strategies, he shared:

> Our frustration with social media was complete, in every avenue. We didn't know how to establish our presence in a really clean, concise way for myself as an individual and D Bar as a restaurant. We just didn't know how to differentiate Keegan the person, Keegan the personality and D Bar the restaurant. We wanted them connected to social media, but we need each to be separate and individual. I was randomly posting on Facebook or answering questions, or tweeting the new schedules, or whatever I liked, but it wasn't really effective. We needed some direction, some focus, to have all integrated in a way that I would get onto everything.

Keegan Gerhard understood the need to segment his different personalities. He continued:

That's a big, big part of social media—to set it up properly so that if I want to say something in the voice of D Bar, I know how to do that. If I want to say something about the Food Network Challenge, I can do that; and if I just want to be Keegan, I can do that. There's not a bunch of crossover, because the crossover is confusing to people and people give up on you if you're not presented properly.

My team understood exactly what he was saying. Confusion is commonplace in social media, especially when the person, company and other activities are merged. One of our goals was to separate the various entities, so that each personality stood on its own.

We recommended flip video cameras be placed on the tables in his restaurants. Customers are encouraged to get creative—to video the food itself, to talk about how much they love the food and report openly on their whole experience at his restaurant.

If patrons submit their video to YouTube, they receive a free dessert next time they come in. (Or whatever the promo that is being offered at that time.) Keegan Gerhard has made this an integral part of what he does—and people love it (*YouTube.com/DBarDesserts*).

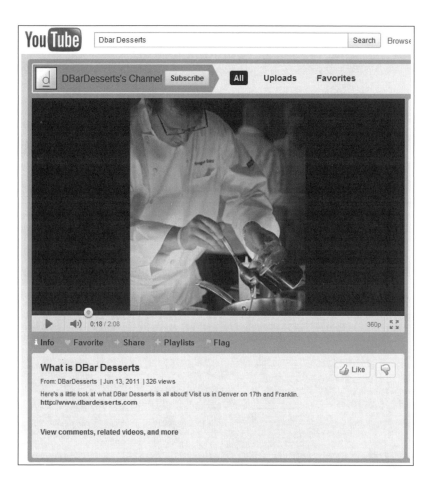

Scan with smartphone to see his
latest video for his restaurant.

Hitting the Hickenlooper Campaign Trail with YouTube

When John Hickenlooper campaigned for Governor of Colorado, he quickly embraced the value of YouTube. He created a series of ads that were fun and uploaded them (*YouTube.com/HickForCo*). He had done ads for his campaigns when he was the Mayor of Denver, but none had the *viral viewership* than his "shower" ad in the Governor's race that focused on negative campaigning and how many just wanted to go take a shower when politicians started the mud-slinging.

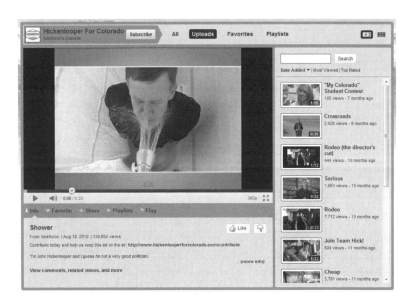

Scan with smartphone to see his latest video for John Hicklooper's channel.

The Governor took the world to the showers with him and won the election in 2010. He added:

> We got emails and tweets from folks all over the country based on that ad. Almost everyone's sick of negative ads.
>
> I've given 10 to 15 years of my life to public service because I think it's important for this country that people believe in government. Social media plays a huge role. It allows us to let people know what's happening and become a partner.

You can read Keegan Gerhard's and Governor John Hickenlooper's full and insightful interviews at:

Findability.com/Thumbonomics10

You'll need to get creative as well, and start thinking, "How can I integrate this into everything I do?"

Since I do so much public speaking, it's pretty easy for me to generate new videos. I use flip video cameras at all my speaking engagements, and capture purely spontaneous feedback as soon as people come out of the event. They receive some kind of freebie for participating.

That's worked really well for my firm. If you look at our YouTube channel, *YouTube.com/HLutze*, you will find a ton of testimonial videos which we repurpose all over the Internet—on our website, on our blogs, etc.

You'll also see videos of invitations to my speaking engagements, which I make for the event promoters. These types of videos help the event planner advertise the events, and really pack the house for my talk.

Uploading a Video to YouTube

When you upload a video on YouTube, (which couldn't be simpler, by the way) you'll be asked for various information. This is where findability comes into play again.

1. **Title the video:** Use a high-value keyword phrase. In this case, whatever title and keyword you use should be appropriate to the actual content of that video.

   Remember the Google AdWords Keyword Tool we talked about in Chapter 5, *Social Media Marketing Keywords for Findability*? Take another look at that tool to choose an appropriate high traffic keyword phrase that fits nicely with each video you do.

2. **Description:** Be as expressive as possible, including the names of everyone appearing in the

video. Describe the content, the situation, and give an idea of who it would appeal to.

3. **List any resources or websites** in the content, in case people want to learn more. You could refer them back to your website or your blog, whatever makes sense for that particular video.

4. **Then it's going to ask for Tags, Category and Thumbnails:** You can actually pick the slice of the video (like a screen photo) that would represent the front that you would see in the YouTube menu, as well as date and location.

5. **Location Tool:** If you're using "Graphic Design, Denver" as your title, or any keyword phrase that has a location modifier in it, make sure you use the location tool in the settings of the video. This will tell Google where the video would rank from a location standpoint.

6. **Transcription of your video's content:** I used a terrific company to transcribe all my books called *CastingWords.com*. Simply send them a link to your YouTube video. They will transcribe the content and send you a Word or HTML document. The cost is minimal and you will be amazed at how your words look in print. This gives you the opportunity to fine-tune what you say on camera in future videos as well as actually having a written script that could be used in a product that your company may want to offer.

As always, the more keyword rich content you feed Google, the better. Here's something to consider:

> Ask people in advance to use a particular keyword when you are interviewing them, or getting any kind of feedback on video. By doing this, you can still keep that spontaneous feel, but get in those all important keywords.

Too Much, Too Little and Just Right

Although you definitely don't need a professional to make videos for YouTube, there is a knack to doing effective ones.

Too much ...

Please don't sit down and read an entire book on YouTube video—try to integrate everything you've learned into a five minute piece. Don't use a lecturing, dissertation style, rambling on and on blandly for a long time. That looks like you are just trying to push out content.

Too little ...

Don't video something totally random that has no possible meaning or connection with your company or your customers. You need to put a bit more thought and effort into it to come up with something relevant to your viewing audience.

Just right ...

Think about what you can produce: videos of events that you are planning, annual meetings, corporate retreats—it can be anything you are willing to share to the public. The main thing is to really exhibit your brand personality.

If your firm is over the top, with an outrageous team of people; you're all about having fun—your videos should convey that. If your firm is very strategic and corporate, your videos should convey that. Whoever you are, there is certainly a place for you on YouTube; but never try to push yourself into a mold that feels uncomfortable.

There is nothing more embarrassing than a corporation trying to be too hip or too cool. You want to be appropriate and authentic at all times in what you do.

Here are three examples of videos I consider too much, too little and just right.

Too little:
http://www.youtube.com/watch?v=RSsQmyprjH8

Watch video now!

Too much:
http://www.youtube.com/watch?v=hTFwMizEdAE

Watch video now!

Just right: Evolution of Dance—Most Watched YouTube Video of All Time!
http://www.youtube.com/watch?v=dMH0bHeiRNg

Watch video now!

Findability Makeover
Go Viral or Not

Recently, I was researching YouTube videos for a presentation I was pulling together on Social Media Findability. I was appalled at the number of embarrassingly bad videos companies were uploading to their channels. I pulled one up about home construction and immediately Enrique Iglesias' "I like it" started playing as audio background for a slide show of showers, decks and siding that started flipping in front of me. The video ended with a blatant endorsement for the web designer who created the video. I wondered, "Could this video be any worse?"

It seems the current goal for most businesses is to "go viral"—two million views equal two million new customers—right? Wrong. Although going viral can be one strategy for your business, you don't have to create a "World of War Craft Freak-Out" video or a collage of people blowing things up in order to have an effective YouTube business strategy.

Problem

We are a professional company, how do we create videos to uphold our brand in YouTube Search and acquire real business leads?

Action Plan

- YouTube is a Search Engine—Treat It Like One!
- Optimize the Key Elements of a Video for Findability
- Key Indicators of Success in YouTube

YouTube Is a Search Engine, Treat It Like One!

When you think about the big search engines, what comes to mind? *Google, Yahoo!, Bing,* maybe even *Ask.com*—right? You may be surprised to learn, as of December 2009, ComScore's US Search Ranking report showed that *YouTube* gets more searches each month than *Yahoo!* or *Bing.* That represents more than 3.9 billion searches in 2009—50 percent more than Yahoo! and 180 percent more than Bing.

It's time to stop thinking about the value of YouTube as simply a video sharing site that your less productive employees are watching, and start treating it like a major Search Engine in your Internet Marketing Strategy.

> Think of every video you create as you would a page on your website—each one will rank and can be found by billions of YouTube searchers.

Every single video you produce and upload to your YouTube Channel should be titled with a high value, highly searched keyword phrase. That's right—you need to treat your YouTube content just like any other content you are creating. You don't need to have baboons juggling bananas—just create great content that your target audience will find interesting, optimize it with keywords that you target audience is searching, and you have the ability to uphold your brand and gain business from YouTube.

Of course, optimizing a YouTube Video is a little different than a webpage. Here is an easy, three-step strategy to Makeover the optimization of your YouTube videos:

Optimize the Key Element of a Video for Findability

1. *Use a Keyword in the Title*: Make sure to research your keywords and use a keyword that is highly searched as part of your naming convention of the

Video Title. Use the *Google Keyword Tool* for researching keyword phrase options: *adwords.google.com/select/KeywordToolExternal*

2. ***Optimize and Create an Effective Description:*** Make sure to have your URL, Call-to-Action or phone number in front of the first sentence in your description. Sprinkle keywords throughout your description for better Findability inside of YouTube.

3. ***Don't Ignore the Keyword Tags:*** Go to *Search Box* in YouTube and you will get suggested searches based on a particular keyword. Example: "Search Engine Marketing" suggestions from YouTube Search Engine Marketing Training, class, help as a more popular alternative. You can use this in your tags as well as in your future video plans for filming. YouTube Video: *youtube.com/watch?v=LZP3GfmoRsg*

You **Tube** | Search Engine Market| | Search |

search engine marketing
search engine marketing **training**
search engine marketing **class**
search engine market**ing help**
search engine marketing **education**
search engine marketing **course**
search engine marketing **for business**
search engine marketing **corporate training**
search engine market**ing conference**
search engine marketing **event**

close

---

4. ***Make Use of Annotations:*** Make sure to use annotation in order to let users know when a video has a more updated version. Link them to a page on your website or blog as well as a clear call to action at the end of the Video. YouTube Video: *youtube.com/watch?v=GU7GGlq-MmE*

Thumbonomics

Of course, it's important to be able to identify what keywords and video content is working. Here are a few metrics you can follow in order to measure your YouTube success meaningfully.

Key Indicators of Success in YouTube

- Increase Subscribers to Your Channel over time
- Number of Total Views
- Getting Found under the Targeted Keyword Phrases in YouTube Search
- Comments on Videos
- YouTube Insight: *youtube.com/watch=?v=Oj2hbcwOaZM*

Track and get detailed information on your videos and watcher behavior such as in the graphics below:

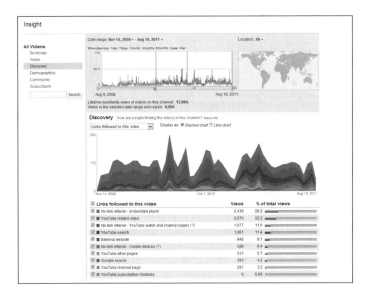

Key Takeaway

Make sure that every ounce of effort you put into your YouTube Channel pays off with views, calls to action and real life business. If you go to the effort to produce videos, then make sure they are getting in front of a searching audience that matters, and will convert to findability and business.

With every video, do your homework and find out how the searcher wants to find that content. Stay connected with how users search, craft your videos around them, and that will get you the visitors and customers you deserve and want. For more information, visit my YouTube Channel at *Youtube.com/HLutze*.

Rule of Thumb

Your YouTube Action Plan ...

1. Set up your YouTube channel with a **high value keyword phrase in the name,** to enhance your official corporate identity and findability.

2. **Fill out the profile with keyword rich content.** Take advantage of every opportunity you have to include a keyword that makes sense and still provides a good user experience.

3. Have your social media committee **pick events coming up for the next year** that are appropriate for video: events, product launches, interviews, upcoming press, conventions, etc. Mark these opportunities on your calendar and make sure you buy

(continued)

enough flip video cameras to actively market these events.

4. **Repurpose existing videos.** Many corporations or companies already have some amount of archived videos. Can you repurpose any of what you have? Perhaps just use a portion of one, or add some more information to another for public viewing? When titling them, always consider which keywords you want those videos to rank under.

5. **Delegate to your social media committee:** Who is going to handle creating new videos at upcoming events? Who is going to optimize existing videos? Who will be in charge of loading them onto YouTube? Set a firm deadline for when these videos need to be uploaded.

6. **Use a high impact visual design** for your YouTube channel. If you get to a certain level, you can become a

Thumbonomics

YouTube channel partner. At that point, they will let you custom design your own look and feel on the channel background.

Until then, you can edit that background to match your corporate colors or put different graphics on it, but there are a limited amount of design features you will be able to do. There are some resources for building a custom YouTube channel. On *YouTube.com* search for "How to make a YouTube Video?" or, "How to setup a YouTube Channel?" and then get ready to learn. You can, of course, search on Google as well.

In closing, YouTube is about having fun, and sharing something in a way that grabs people's interest completely differently than pure textual content does. YouTube lets you start to express your corporate personality. Not only will you create pieces that showcase the best of who you

(continued)

are, they could easily go viral. Popular videos are passed on rapidly from person to person, that's part of the fun; part of the exciting potential of the thing.

Remember, you don't need to be a professional videographer. People simply love video and the spontaneity of it. There isn't a day that goes by that someone does not send me a link to a YouTube video that they think is amazing, hilarious, thought-provoking—in other words, I need to see it. Frequently, I send them on to others as well ... don't you?

This is probably a very different modality than you are used to—therefore, keep it easy and fun. If you do, YouTube will definitely take you to a whole new place for your corporate marketing objectives. Most people are visual; don't miss out on using this free form of communicating with millions.

You just finished this chapter. Congratulations! Now tell us what you think, the tools you use and get additional offers and giveaways. Scan this QR Code with your smartphone or go to *Findability.com/Thumbonomics10* for more YouTube insights. You will also have access to the full Audio and PDF downloads of the FULL INTERVIEWS with Keegan Gerhard and Governor John Hickenlooper. There is good stuff in these LIVE interviews. Don't miss out!

11

Blogging Findability

Move Your Business Forward with Relevant, Content-Rich Blogging

Does blogging qualify as social media at all? This is hotly contested in our office. Some think blogging is the strongest and most immediately effective social media platform there is. Others argue that blogs are great, but are not social media ... they think blogs are like Internet magazines that have a variety of articles.

Whichever you believe, the important thing to consider is that blogs are highly regarded by search engines as a more relevant, current, continuous source of content than websites. As I mentioned in the Introduction to *Thumbonomics*, even the best websites tend to be stagnant, non-changing entities, whereas blogs tend to be constantly changing and new content rich.

I've been talking about blogs with my clients for years. Many of them initially said, "I just don't have that kind of time; perhaps I will get around to it later." Others set up a blog, but never actually wrote anything ... and others start one, only to abandon it within weeks.

Well, it is later … and *now is the time to do it …*

Now is the time to start actively and aggressively blogging. It's time to get busy.

Does Anyone Actually Read Blogs?

In a word: Yes! Here are the stats: 33 percent of Internet users read blogs, which translates into 346 million people globally. That's major! If you can imagine it, two new blogs are created every second. There is tremendous interest. The bottom line for any leader: don't miss this marketing and branding opportunity.

You don't like blogs personally, and, never read them? As I keep saying, it is not helpful in terms of moving your business forward to judge how people want to receive their information. Huge numbers of people absolutely love blogs.

Why? Because blogs are content rich, and easily available. Most blogs can be subscribed to via an RSS feed. That stands for "Really Simple Syndication." If you subscribe to a blog in this manner, you will receive an automatic update in your inbox or homepage every time there is a new entry to that blog.

With RSS feeds, you can have a continuous stream of content on subjects you are interested in, need to learn about, or are simply entertained by—automatically delivered to you. What could be more perfect in today's hectic, modern world?

Where to House Your Blog

The well known real estate phrase, "location, location, location," is critical for your host website. The wrong one can lead to extreme levels of frustration, and sometimes, disaster. One of our clients is a theatrical manuscript company that built an external blog—meaning a blog that was off their own domain. It was "hosted" by someone else. When we started working with them, they had 400 to 500 different manuscripts on their externally hosted blog. They had already moved their Blog BEFORE we started working with them. They had lost 50 percent in sales and traffic—which equaled millions of dollars in lost revenues.

From the beginning, the original company hosting their blog knew how inextricably bound the manuscript company was to the traffic in their blog posts. It was a major part of their business, accounting for a significant amount of their traffic and sales. Subsequently, every year, the hosting company would raise their rates. They knew they had this company between a rock and a hard spot.

Starting with one blogging host doesn't mean that you are stuck with them for life. Google how to move a blog for a variety of references. If you have a savvy webmaster, he or she can do it as well.

Sites like Blogger aren't recommended, although they are probably the biggest and most popular one out there. Using Blogger is tempting, since it's so simple to set up, and of course, it's free. However, I encourage you to build a blog that's housed inside your own domain, reflecting your corporate brand. By doing this, you'll build brand recognition and back links to your blog.

Your domain will receive value in the search engines each time people use the link to your blog, attached to your website. Once you have subscribers, all these people clicking on your blog adds up to something meaningful that builds credibility and value for your own website, not for someone else's.

If I subscribe to a blog hosted on Blogger, each time I'm notified of a new post, and click on that link, I am increasing Blogger's popularity and ranking in the search engines. You want to increase your own.

Setting Up Your Blog for Optimum Findability

Naming your blog can be tricky, and requires some serious consideration.

Scan with your smartphone to go to Duct Tape Marketing website.

When I first started following blogs, there was one called Duct Tape Marketing (*DuctTapeMarketing.com/blog*) that was

Thumbonomics

devoted to all types of marketing. If you somehow got them to post about you, it instantly increased your credibility—it was seen all over the Internet. Duct Tape Marketing has over 120,000 followers.

When you name your blog, make sure it is keyword rich. No surprise there … Let's use our fictitious graphic design company, Go Creative, as an example. Go Creative can go two different ways in naming their blog:

- As a sub-domain, *GoCreativeGraphicDesignBlog. MyDomain.com*
- Or, *YourDomainName.com/GoCreativeGraphic DesignBlog*

Don't worry about the title being too long for people to remember. People don't often type in blog names; usually they click on blog links right inside your website or from an external link they saw on search results. Whatever the title, the more keyword rich it is, the more findable it is and the better your blog will work for you overall.

Blog formatting is also important to consider. The Findability Group is currently using *WordPress.com* for all of our blogs, and recommending it to all our clients.

WordPress contains a treasure trove of good designers, advanced features, and gorgeous themes.

Advantages of WordPress:

- We love WordPress because it is completely **open source**, and improves continually. An open source technology means there are many people out there building a better and better product over time— for free.
- Anytime you want to **change the look and feel** of your blog, you just have to change the "skin," like painting a room with different color. WordPress allows you to replace the skin without completely rebuilding the blog. This is an amazing advantage, because you will get tired of the look and feel of your blog after a year or two.
- It's a **super simple interface and very easy to use**. You can log in through your Internet connection or your mobile phone. You can add and edit posts as easily as you would edit a Word document.

Other blog formats include WordPad and Drupal. There are many others out there as well, but at the Findability Group, our preference at this writing is WordPress.

Blogs Are About Content!

When writing content for a blog, always consider your readers first and the search engines second. I know it's tempting to load tons of keywords into your posts. Please don't do that. Nothing is more jarring and off-putting to a reader than to have keywords repeated over and over, when they don't really add anything to the content. It's such an obvious ploy. Be mindful of the reader, write something of genuine value or interest to them—then *sprinkle* in keywords appropriate to the content.

Make good use of keyword tools, such as the *Google Adwords* or *KeywordDiscovery.com.* If you have an idea for a post, check one of these sites and see how people search that particular topic. Then start writing around the main keyword phrases you discover. That will help you craft a keyword rich blog post that is easily found by the searching public, and relevant to search engines.

Similar to pages on a website, each post on your blog is ranked individually by Google. The blog as a whole is ranked by its individual pieces, called blog posts. Each post may need different keywords, depending on its topic.

Many people have the misconception that a blog is an unendingly long dissertation that goes on and on. I've heard it a million times …

- I don't have time for that.
- I'm not a writer.

And the biggie,

- I have nothing to blog on.

A blog post can be any length. It can simply be a photograph or video, with a paragraph explaining it. Longer is not necessarily better. With the rapid increase in the use of Twitter, blogs have actually shortened in length—it's common to read just a few paragraphs vs. a full blown article format.

Blogging ideas to consider include what's happening at your company on a daily, monthly and yearly level. I'll bet there are all sorts of things happening at your company every day you can blog on. Such as:

- Do you have visitors coming? Any company events?
- Do you put out press releases?
- Do you attend corporate and annual meetings, or conventions?
- How about announcing new products, or products in development?
- Has one of your employees identified a cost saving technique?
- Why not respond to events in your industry, or related industries? If something is happening in your industry, put your voice "into the ring" and talk about that.

These all provide wonderful blogging opportunities. Whenever anyone in your company goes to a conference, they can blog about what they learned there. If you have a booth at a convention, make sure to leverage that to the fullest ...

Come visit us at Booth 600.
Meet the CEO and get a free gift.

Conventions and conferences are a wonderful place to subscribe more people to your blog as well.

Consider doing guest interviews. When I first started blogging, I did podcasts whenever I was at a convention. I would pull two or three of the convention's speakers aside, and interview them.

Then I would post the MP3 of the interview on my blog, with a picture of the speaker, a short bio and brief summary of what we talked about. In this way, I attracted a huge amount of followers very quickly. This allowed blogging to become an important part of my business over time.

Jettison the idea that blogging is only for "real writers," or that blog posts need to be long, wordy dissertations. Instead, look for blogging opportunities in everything your company does—I guarantee you will find them.

Blogs Are Informational Tools for Your Customers

Your blog can be used to help people through their buying process. For example, if you have an expensive purchase, one that takes a long time over a series of meetings to buy, you can walk customers through the buying process with a series of educational blogs. This is a fantastic way to educate the consumer, provide true value and show your expertise. Let them know what is so different about your product or service. You shine as a result. Suggested topics include:

- How to pick a vendor.
- How to tell exceptional quality.

- Pitfalls to watch out for.
- How to go out for RFPs or ask for proposals within certain industries.

Who Will Do the Actual Writing?

Ahhh, always a key question: who is going to be the creator of the words? Your initial goal is to keep a keyword rich, (but not over the top) consistent level of blogging over a month's time.

Can you commit to that, as a company? Who will be the official blogger for your company? You, your social media brand manager, someone on the social media committee? Do you want one voice only, or will you mix it up and allow various staff members to add posts?

Once you commit to an ongoing blog, meet with your social media committee. Decide which departments should be involved. One effective way to go about it is to create a schedule for blog posts, along with a list of topics and ideas. Assign those posts in advance, with a firm due date. Repeat this meeting once a month. In this way, you will always have new material for the blog on an ongoing basis.

A beginning blog might use content only. An advanced blogger would post five or more times a month and incorporate video components, podcasts (audio MP3 recordings), and guest bloggers (experts they invite to come in and blog on their behalf).

There are all different kinds of interesting and effective blogs out there.

Blogging Pitfalls

- Please, whatever you do—don't just copy and paste your website content into a blog post. That's a no-no. Google does not want to see duplicate content between websites and blog posts.
- I'm sure I don't have to tell you not to copy other people's posts or website content.
- Stay away from hard sales pitches. The blog is where you want to be conversational, informational or educational—not sales oriented.
- No promotions, promotional ads and fliers. They have their place in your marketing strategy—but they don't belong in a blog.

Blog Components, from the Findability Standpoint

1. **Titling the Blog:** Yes, put in the keyword phrase that fits the best, preferably toward the front of your title.

    If you're blogging about findability articles, the title would be: findability articles, colon, and a catchy, creative phrase after that.

    For example, *Findability Articles: Where are they when you need them?*

    I can't tell you how many times I have seen blog posts with wonderful, creative titles—creative titles that will never be found by search engines. Why? Because the titles are so obscure in nature they cannot be ranked. No search engine knows what they are about.

Remember—you must tell Google where to put it before anyone can find it and read it. You do that using a keyword phrase.

2. **Keyword Density:** Two to five percent keyword density is perfect for the body of the post. Imagine, "sprinkling" your keywords in, as opposed to "flooding" the article with them.

    There's a wonderful website called *Wordle.net*. It can show you what's called a pictorial word graph. You'll be able to see how many times you have used specific words and then you can "see" what you're saying to the search engine.

    It would be highly educational to put the keywords in your blog post into *Wordle* and see what information you get back; you'll quickly see if you're on the right track.

3. **Link Out:** Google wants you to be a credible source of blogging. It expects experts to link to experts. Put links inside the body of your blog taking the reader to the different content, people, and reference sites you're writing about. If you learned something from an expert at a convention, link out to both the expert's site and the convention's site.

4. **Tags and Post Descriptions:** Inside WordPress, you'll see there's a place for tags. These are simply descriptive keywords about what the blog is about.

(Findability, articles, conventions, etc.) You will also have a place to add a short excerpt description summarizing what the post is about. Make sure to use keywords in the excerpt description as well.

5. **Comments:** Now, the fun begins! A lot of people really get nervous about comments, but they are what makes your blog into a conversation. Comments may not happen right away. Do you remember the movie *Julie and Julia* starring Meryl Streep? It took many weeks before Julie Powell's food blog got its first comment. Titled *The Julie/Julia Project*, within months, it was the buzz of the country, which in turn led to a significant book deal and movie starring Meryl Streep. It all started with a blog.

   Over time, if you are really putting relevant content out, you will start to get more readers, blog loyalty, and more and more comments. Set up the blog so the comments wait in a staging area; they don't immediately go live on your blog. Remember, these comments will just sit there until you approve them, delete them or mark them as spam, so check for comments every day.

   You will probably get a considerable amount of spam. For every three to four comments I get on my blogs, one to two are spam. That's to be expected; it's no reflection on the quality of your posts or blog as a whole. It only means there are a lot of people out there who don't know better.

They think putting blog comments with a link back to their site will help their search engine optimization efforts (which it doesn't).

Delete spam immediately; be careful with what you allow on your blog. Start encouraging your existing customer base to participate in creating the conversation. One way to increase blog readership is to invite all your clients, prospects, and colleagues to subscribe to your blog.

You also might want to have multiple blogs on your website: one that appeals to prospects and one that appeals to your current client base. You speak to them differently because their education/buying cycle is different and their needs are different.

Be vigilant about the "voice" of your blogs. Know who it is you are trying to reach. I've got three different blogs: one for my books; one for my public speaking and one for the consulting business.

The Blogging Action Plan

1. **Establish your blogging platform.** Consider *WordPress.com* or *TypePad.com*. Choose one that is open source and has plug-ins. Plug-ins are a way

of adding technology and add-ons over time without great expense. On WordPress, plug-ins are updated over time as is the whole WordPress system itself—and it's all free!

2. **Have the blog "ported" into your website** *(meaning installed into your website).* Your web developer or IT department can easily do this. You definitely don't want it to be external to your domain. Check out the available plug-ins, and add them as well.

3. **Once the blog is set up on your site, add a tab to your website's primary navigation.** *Readers can simply click on the tab to read the blog, the same way they would click on "home" or "contact us."* It's really important to integrate that up front.

4. **Have your web team create a "skin" or a design theme that's consistent with the look and feel of your website.** *When people jump from your website to your blog, they don't feel like they've been taken somewhere different.* You want a nice consistency between the two.

5. **Whoever will be doing the actual posting should have a tutorial from your web team on how to navigate WordPress's content management system.** It's quite simple; no programming knowledge or technical knowledge required. It's literally as easy as writing a Word document, and can be delegated to someone else in the office when you go on vacation.

6. **Write good posts, giving content your readers will love and can really use.** This is the key to blogging success.

7. **Use a keyword phrase in the title based on the post's topic.** Use those Google keyword tools we talked about earlier in Chapter 5, *Social Media Marketing Keywords for Findability*. Stick to a keyword plan for every single blog post.

8. **Sprinkle your keyword phrases throughout the body of the post.** Remember—if you don't tell Google where to put it, it won't turn up in a search, and your potential readers will never find it.

   Great blogging is twofold—you want your content to provide a good reader experience, as well as a good search engine outcome.

9. **Add other media.** A blog post needs to be visually interesting, just like your website. Add relevant photos that you have taken, or use *images.google.com* or *stockphoto.com*. There are many different websites providing good stock photography, stock imagery, or clip art ... adding another level of visual interest to the content of that blog. Videos are always great too. (Are you starting to get ideas as to how your different social media platforms can work together?)

10. **Post and monitor comments weekly.** Once you post to the blog, start monitoring your comments. They will arrive as an email notification. You can

approve them, delete them, or mark them as spam … whichever is appropriate.

Keep in mind that you won't have a huge influx of comments right out of the gate. I've had my blog for three years now. It takes time to really build momentum and get a blogging community that's really engaged and commenting on your blogs. Hopefully, you are in it for the long haul, and it will pay off.

You're invited to visit my blogs: You can visit my blog at *Findability.com/blog*. This one blog encapsulates the consulting, speaking and university sections of my website.

Scan with your smartphone to go to *Findability.com/blog*

So, start blogging! You've put it off long enough. You know you should have done it two years ago, but no matter. Don't look back; look ahead—and now is the time. And, when your blog is up, let me know!

Findability Makeover
Blogging:
Better than Flipping a Sign on the Corner

Blogging … anyone heard of it? Or have you been ignoring it since you first heard this word years ago? Search engines seek out non-spammy, trusted sources of content for as long as I have been in search engine marketing. Blogs are that source of high quality, keyword-rich content. I speak to groups all over the US on content building strategies and best practices for SEM. I am consistently amazed by the deer-in-the-headlight responses I still get from business owners to the concept of blogging.

Blogging is probably one of the most powerful platforms outside of your website to get recognition as a content matter expert. Findability is about showing up to search engines as the "professor" or content expert in your field. How do professors prove they are the real thing? They publish.

Search engines are looking for content that is keyword rich and high quality. Blogs meet that expectation post after post. If you are going to blog on a regular basis, whether it is monthly or weekly, make sure that every ounce of effort that goes into each blog post is utilized for maximum Findability.

Business owners might start taking this medium more seriously if they see the instant impact their blog has to represent them in search results, as well as inside of social media sites when users search inside those portals.

Problem

If I, as a business owner, have put off blogging, but am now ready to tackle it—how can I make the most of every post for search and overall Findability?

Action Plan

- Use *LSIKeywords.com* or Google Adwords Contextual Targeting Tool for keyword ideas and post inspiration.
- Write blog posts with keyword rich titles and content.
- Track your results in Google and Social Media Sites for Ultimate Findability.

Action #1: Use LSI Keywords for Keyword Ideas and Post Inspiration

LSI is short for Latent Semantic Indexing and is an important part of your SEO strategy and Findability. This site is one of those "inside" tools that most search marketing professionals know about and recommend. It's essential for the search marketer's arsenal. Use it.

Resource

LSIKeywords.com is a tool that shows related search terms to the current search query. You can also use the tool Contextual Targeting Tool assuming you have a Google Adwords account (*google.com/adwords*). Both of these tools will help you to define highly relevant keywords for your blog titles. To discover fully how to use the Google Adwords Contextual Targeting Tool, go to:

youtube.com/watch?v=eBYtfXzZl0c

 **Scan to watch this video.**

Example: Internet Marketing Denver

I like our agency to be found locally. To accomplish this, I need to know how people search for us, or related searches, so I can come up with blog post after blog post that has different content, but helps extend my reach to the local areas like Denver, Colorado, etc. I start by putting my topic idea "Internet Marketing Denver" into LSIKeywords.

LSI means Latent Semantic Indexing. *LSIKeywords.com* explains their service directly from their website:

> This tool searches the top 10 in Google for a phrase you like to rank highly for. Then it collects all the text from these 10 result pages and calculates the most used words and phrases on these pages. It then orders them by number of times used. With this data you know exactly why these pages rank highly in Google. It's all about theming and using LSI Keywords. For more proof and info about this subject, read further.

You will find this to be an amazing tool!

When sitting down to write blog posts week after week, this tool will keep your ideas connected with all the different ways people search for your type of business. It will increase your chances of having your blog found outside of your own website and have your posts represent your business in search results and social media sites.

Action #2: Write Blog Posts
with Keyword-Rich Titles and Body Text

Scan to see Sign Flipper video!
youtube.com/watch?v=eHlwSHL1gxk

Just like those people who stand on the corner flipping a signboard around, trying to entice you into buying a sandwich or car wash, it helps to consider every blog post as an opportunity to get your company noticed in search results. Once you get clear on the keywords as explained in Action #1, then you are ready to write. Make sure to use the EXACT keyword phrase at the front of your blog post **Internet Marketing Denver** and then use a "dash" to connect the keyword with the creative idea.

Post Title: Internet Marketing Denver—Google's Newest App, Google Cloud Connect.

Then spread the keyword of the article throughout the body copy without disrupting user experience, while not being spammy and repeating the same keywords over and over.

Subscribe

Internet Marketing Denver - Google's Newest App, Google Cloud Connect

Newest Google App Allows Easy Syncing Between Cloud & Microsoft Office

It was announced via the Official Google Blog today that their newest service, Google Cloud Connect, is out of beta and available to the public.

Google Cloud Connect is a toolbar for Microsoft Office that you can download that automatically installs to all of your Microsoft Office applications. You must first connect it to a Google account, but the toolbar remembers your info and you are able to switch accounts easily at any time. You will then be able to sync your documents to Google Docs so you constantly have an online backup of your files. Also, and this is the really cool feature, you can share your Office documents with colleagues so you can all be editing the same document at the same time. Much like in the online version of Google Docs, when two or more people are editing a document at the same time, those changes will automatically appear on everyone's desktop document.

This eliminates the need for emailing multiple versions of the same document which almost always leads to confusion. Google Cloud Connect not only will sync your Office Word documents, but PowerPoint presentations and spreadsheets as well. Internet Marketing Denver firm Findability Group recommends you download this free toolbar and give it a shot! You'd be amazed at how much time and frustration cloud computing will save you.

You can download Google Cloud Connect and watch some other videos explaining how to use this feature here. Being a Google app, you can rest assured that downloading and installation is fast and extremely easy.

For more internet marketing Denver news, be sure to follow the Findability Group on Twitter and Facebook!

Action #3: Track Your Results in Search Engines and Social Media

Google Analytics & Facebook insights will help you evaluate whether your blogs are getting real traction outside of your own blog. If you use Action steps 1 and 2 correctly, you will not only generate traffic and subscribers to your own blog, but you'll be findable under your chosen keyword phrase (for instance "Internet marketing Denver") in search results and social media sites like Facebook.

Here's the bottom line: You have waited long enough, now is the time to blog. I have given you three ways to help improve the content, Findability and tracking of each blog post. Make sure you are getting the most out of each blog and make sure it is optimized for a keyword phrase to *flip a sign* for your business in search results.

As you continue to blog, search engines will recognize you for the experts you are and you will get the exposure your business deserves.

Rule of Thumb

Blogging is a significant player in your social media strategy. It allows the writer/owner to present thoughts and concepts in a more detailed format than Twitter, Facebook and LinkedIn. Most companies have a tab on the Home page of their websites that identifies their blog and encourages email signups for receiving future blogs as they are posted. Your blog becomes an instant forum to reach out to your customers in communicating news.

You just finished this chapter. Congratulations! Now tell us what you think, the tools you use, and get additional offers and giveaways. Scan this QR Code with your smartphone or go to *Findability.com/Thumbonomics11* for more blogging insights.

12

Mobile Marketing:
The Other Computer

Smart Phones: No Longer Just Phones, They're Your Mobile Marketing Window on the World

Josh Alves, used with permission

A while back, I spoke at the Online Marketing Summit (OMS) in San Diego. Perhaps one month prior to that engagement, I had posted some very kind words about an organization called Denver Hospice to my Facebook account. My dad had recently passed away, and this organization had been an incredible help throughout the whole process for me and my family.

At the end of OMS, a woman came up to me and handed me her business card. I stood there in shock, because her card said, *"Creative Director for the Denver Hospice."*

Remember, I am based in Denver, but this was San Diego. I must have had a stunned look on my face, causing her to ask, *"Are you OK?"*

I replied, *"I'm just so surprised to meet you in San Diego."* Her response was revealing ...

I was originally going to attend a different session, but when I went to your Facebook profile on my phone, there was your wonderful praise of Denver Hospice. I knew I had to come and hear you instead.

An amazing connection resulted from my posting to Facebook—and this woman accessing Facebook in the moment, on the spot, via her mobile phone.

The point I want to make is that smartphones are no longer just phones. They should probably be called mobile computers; they have become so incredibly sophisticated. People are now using smartphones as their "other computer."

I think one of the reasons smartphones are so popular (and why mobile marketing should be a part of your 2011-2012 marketing plan) comprises three key factors:

1. **Efficiency:** Think about it ... Your smartphone is always with you. It allows for a spontaneous sharing of whatever's happening to you in that very moment.

2. **Immediacy:** You can connect quickly. Do it fast; get it done right now ...
3. **Convenience:** No jotting down memos or making mental notes to post later, on your PC, when you are back at the office. You probably always have your cell phone with you. Simply whip it out, record the moment, and move on to the next one.

Social Media and the 20s and 30s? A Natural!

I had an interesting conversation with Natalie Henley in my office. The topic—exactly what is it about cell phones, tweeting, Facebooking and texting for 20-somethings? Why are they so obsessed with it?

Natalie, who is in her mid-twenties, shared a fascinating insight with me—one that put her generation's enthusiasm for these modern technologies in perfect perspective:

My life matters and my opinion matters—and it matters hour-to-hour, minute-to-minute, second-to-second.

She went on to share that her friends' self-identify in the moment and that their belief was that the over-30s are more judgmental of how they live and use social media. From their perspective, it's an "adapt or die" philosophy.

If you're over the age of, say, 40, this may be a very, very foreign concept to you. Why would anyone want to post, the instant it's happening, something they're seeing or doing ... something they're experiencing ... a food they're eating … a thought they are having …? And why would anyone else want to read it?

This difference in perspective creates a huge dichotomy in how younger generations use technology, compared to older generations. Embracing this new perspective makes all the difference between being on the cutting edge of marketing today, or playing catch-up.

A New Perspective

Mobile marketing may not be comfortable for you. You might find it distracting, incomprehensible and perhaps even inconvenient. But it's absolutely what is comfortable and convenient for 20- and 30-somethings.

As this user-base comes up in age and earning capacity, they will begin purchasing more and more products and services. If you attract this market today, these people will buy from your company now and after you've retired or handed the business off to your kids. To capitalize on that, your business needs to be front and center—ready to engage them meaningfully, in the way that *they want to engage*.

If your attitude toward mobile marketing is, "I don't do that, so I'm not going to do that for my company."—get over it! If you do get over your dislike or incomprehension of mobile marketing, you might just discover that there's a huge fun factor in it.

There are now hundreds of thousands of apps, between the Droid and the iPhone platforms. You can find an app for just about anything from snow reports, playing games, stocks, weather, generating a light saber, finding a restaurant, tracking miles-per-gallon, travel, to-do lists, barcode scanners, coupon finders, even turning your voice into a cartoon sound—just about anything you can imagine, there's an app out there.

A new phone these days is equivalent to a fabulous new toy. This perception does not exist in quite the same way with a computer. A computer equals work for many of us. In contrast, a smartphone equals fun, connection, entertainment, and excitement.

Consider the perspective of enthusiastic mobile users; those who are using this technology to validate that their lives are meaningful:

I want to have fun with my life, and I want to share all these great, fun moments with you. And you. And you.

The mobile marketing process is accelerating rapidly, at an entirely different rate than with the use of traditional computers. You still must brand to prospects through social media, but mobile is the catalyst that can move it forward at light speed.

Before, we thought, "OK, yeah, I'll post that on Facebook when I get to the office." Now it's being done in the moment, as it happens. This has changed everything about the timeliness of social media.

How fast does a post age? How long is data really relevant? Is it only relevant for five minutes after you've posted it? Does it have any kind of shelf life at all?

The communities we feed through mobile want a continuous amount of meaningful content fed to them. They want to engage, and be engaged. Here are some suggestions as to how to do that …

Mobile Marketing's Big Three

1. *Yelp.com*

 I've been intrigued by Yelp and its growth, for quite a while. It started out as mainly restaurant reviews, but now is for reviews of any type of business or service. If you're not already on Yelp, please sign up for a business account and *unlock* your business.

Why? Because over 39 million people visited Yelp in November 2010 alone—to post reviews, and help them decide where to spend their money.

To help business owners get the most out of their online presence, Yelp offers a suite of free tools, tools to:

- Communicate with your customers—privately and publicly.
- Track how many people view your business page.
- Add photos, a detailed business description, up-to-date information, history, and specialties.
- Announce special offers and upcoming events.
- Recommend other businesses.

Keyword Findability Inside of Yelp

Like social media sites Facebook and Twitter, Yelp is a search engine. Unfortunately, when I set up my Yelp account a year and a half ago, I made the silly mistake of not applying my own principles. (Hate to admit it; but you can learn from my mistake!)

What did I do wrong? I set up the name of the company as *Findability Group.* I could just as easily have used the full description—*Findability Group Search Marketing*—but I didn't. Consequently, if you put "search marketing" into Yelp's search box—you won't find my company.

When you set up your Yelp account, *put your most important key word or phrase right in your name.*

Fortunately, I can use keywords throughout my Yelp profile, so I still have some Findability. When setting up the description of your business or service, make sure you use keywords in the profile section. When someone searches Yelp with keyword phrases that aren't based on your company name, they will still be able to find you in a meaningful way.

Still feeling vague about how Yelp actually works?

I searched "authentic dim sum Denver" inside Yelp. The first name that came up was a local Chinese restaurant named *Star Kitchen*. Clearly, the name *Star Kitchen* does not have "dim sum" or "authentic" in it, so why did it come up first?

I started looking at their reviews. It turned out; many of the reviews actually had "authentic dim sum" in the text. Yelp was searching all the reviews for dim sum, as well as the names of restaurants. When they found Star

Kitchen's reviews with that wording, they shuffled it to the top of the page.

Let Your Customers Market For You

Start by encouraging people who already love your products or services to review you on Yelp. Every time a client, customer or business associate gives you positive feedback, ask them if they would go onto Yelp, set up a personal account, and praise your company.

Why would they be willing to do all that work? To the vast array of people who love connecting with social and mobile media—it's not work—it's fun. It's what they like to do anyway!

In a perfect world, you would be able to "coach" your reviewers to use specific keywords in their reviews. That's probably not practical, but if you are already asking loyal customers to post a review, why not mention a couple of key words you would like included in their postings?

2. Foursquare.com

 This innovative site is really about location based push marketing. If you have not heard of them, this is how they describe themselves:

Foursquare is a mobile application that makes cities easier to use and more interesting to explore. It is a friend-finder, a social city guide and a game that challenges users to experience new things, and rewards them for doing so. Foursquare lets users "check in" to a place when they're there, tell friends where they are, track the history of where they've been and who they've been there with.

To use Foursquare, simply set up an account and claim your business. Make sure to load your venue page with all kinds of interesting tidbits about your company. Make a special VIP offer to anyone who *checks in with you.*

How Does It Work?

If you are wondering why someone would *check in* with a business, here's how it works:

I went to the Marriot for a few days to work on this book. As soon as I got there I got out my phone, went onto Foursquare and *checked in* with Sonoma's, the restaurant in the Marriot. Then, I went back and took a look at *TweetEffect.com* that was mentioned in Chapter 13, *Productivity Tools*. As a result of checking in at Sonoma's, I got two additional Twitter followers.

Right across the street from the Marriott is a Chili's restaurant. When I *checked in* to the Marriot in Foursquare, Chili's knew I was across the street. I could see their special offer as well—free chips and salsa with *check-in*.

My team has decided to have dinner at Chili's and actually check-in and see if they honor the offer they've put in Foursquare. We talked with our waitress who shared that they get from six to ten chips and salsa requests from Foursquare check-ins per shift.

Can you use Foursquare for other purposes besides offering deals for your business? Absolutely!

Foursquare became a fixture of John Hickenlooper's campaign for Governor in Colorado in 2010. He was introduced to it by a friend's son—a friend with whom he had opened a brewery pub back in the 90s. He was told:

> When you're campaigning, here's this thing called Foursquare. A lot of people don't know about it yet; hardly anybody uses it. But, it's perfect for what you want to do. I think it's going to explode and think you should get on board with it now.

Sage advice for all politicians—have Internet whiz kids in marketing as part of your team! For Hickenlooper, it paid off as he reached out to the residents throughout the state—wherever he was, he used Foursquare to let anyone find him using the GPS on their cell phones.

Foursquare has a fun feature called *mayorships* (in Yelp they're called *dukedoms*). Foursquare *mayorships* are awarded to your customers with the most days *checked into* your venue over the last 60 days.

Someone could be the Mayor of Chili's, or the Mayor of your business! The mayor is seen right on your Foursquare Venue page, and always gets a special gift—a free order of fries, a book or whatever promotion you can offer them. Whether you are a B2B, or a non-restaurant or storefront type business, you can still offer users something just for *checking in*.

While I was searching for Chili's, I was able to see other companies in the surrounding area as well, as long as they had a Foursquare account. So why not have one? Tens of thousands of venues are currently experimenting with special offers on Foursquare.

People use Foursquare as a search engine for local products and services. Why search for local businesses in

Foursquare instead of just Googling? Again—because it's fun, modern, interactive and you get user reviews right away.

Whether you feel like Foursquare relates to your own business or not, you'll still want to be findable inside this rapidly growing Internet community. Once you have a Foursquare Venue page, make sure to update your community on a regular basis about what's happening within your company.

3. QR codes

 QR (quick response) codes connect the digital world with the real world. Similar to a digital thumbprint, a QR Code is a specific two-dimensional code, readable by smartphones and camera phones. The code consists of black modules arranged in a square pattern on a white background. The information encoded can be text, URL, or any other data.

What do you do with a QR code?

They can be used like a treasure hunt. You can put them all over—in magazines, on print materials, business cards, websites, blogs, or in the window of your business. A user scans this code with their smartphone. They might be taken to your website, see a message from your business, or instantly receive a promotional offer.

Thumbonomics

You can drive users to Yelp, Twitter and Facebook with QR codes. They are becoming increasingly popular because they give the user a unique experience or offer that no one else would receive. They allow users to interact with your company in a way that's meaningful and engaging—like playing a game together, if you will.

If you Google *"QR code generator,"* you will find a slew of sites to make these codes. I like the QR Code generator *QRcode.good-survey.com*. I used this tool for all the QR codes in this book.

There's also a more advanced technology called JAGTAG you might want to take a look at. When someone scans the JAGTAG, it actually sends a video you have created back to their phone. And people absolutely love videos! Go to *Jagtag.com* for more information.

QR Codes are not a new convention, but they seem to be making a big comeback. Scan a QR code with your mobile phone and you'll receive instant information on the company as well as website addresses and more. This technology may be a bit *passé* to the geek in your life, but it's a very effective way of getting real, localized action for your business.

At the Findability Group, we use a QR Code on coffee mugs, t-shirts at conferences, etc. When you scan the QR Code, it takes you straight to our blog post on QR Codes at *http://www.findability.com/uncategorized/what-qr-code-mobile-marketing-strategy.*

Groupon—A Mobile Marketing Success Story

 Are you familiar with *Groupon.com*? Groupon was founded in November, 2008, with the slogan "Get it, Share it, Enjoy it!" At $0 in revenues when it opened its doors, Groupon reached $2.5 billion in less than four years. Has that gotten your attention?

It usually offers one deal a day per city. Local merchants contract with Groupon to offer their products or services at a substantial discount to its email subscribers (in the 50 percent area) and on Facebook and Twitter feeds. If a specific number of subscribers buy the Groupon coupon deal that the merchant has identified as the "minimal number of participants needed," the deal is on. How does Groupon make money?—it gets 50 percent of what is paid—it's a cash cow.

In December of 2010, the owners rejected a six billion dollar buyout from Google. Declining six billion dollars (!) shows the tremendous effort and commitment the owners have put into this business, and their belief in becoming independently successful. That's pretty impressive right there …

But what's even more impressive to me is the way Groupon has used mobile and social media marketing to build this incredible brand.

Groupon offers one "deal of the day," each day. As I write this, today's offer is with a local pizzeria—$25 worth of pizza for only $12. When I rechecked it a few hours later, the offer already had 770 redemptions. This means 770 people (at least) will go to this particular pizza parlor with their Groupon voucher, and pay $12 to get pizza that would ordinarily cost them $25.

The pizza merchant will get an enormous amount of new business—people who will talk about his pizza and his pizza parlor, and perhaps become repeat customers. The revenue brought in by this special offer is split with Groupon.

Remember, their slogan was "Get it, Share it, Enjoy it." They use good, incentivized offers and make it oh-so-easy to share. You receive their latest offer on your mobile phone every morning. And you'll pass it on to everyone you know who loves pizza, or whatever the latest offer is—because it is such great deal.

There is a Groupon app for the Droid and the iPhone. I, as a Groupon member, can log right into my Groupon app, no matter where I am across the U.S. and see the local offer for that day.

Because the offers are so limited (today only!), there's a bit of a feeding frenzy around them. People feel the urgency to act now and get in on it. They don't want to miss out. And they share it freely, saying, "Hurry, get this. It's a great deal" to everyone they know who might be interested. Groupon is super easy to share on Facebook and Twitter.

Why am I telling you about Groupon? They are a prime example of a company that got on board early with mobile marketing. They "got it." They shared it. Apparently they plan to continue enjoying it …

Wouldn't you want to be so successful, and have so much potential, that you are given the chance to decline a six billion dollar payout?

I certainly can't guarantee that will ever happen. But, whether your company gets that big or not, I suggest you embrace mobile marketing with great energy and great respect for the potential of this technology. If you can't quite believe mobile marketing is your next step, please at least keep it in mind—your competitors undoubtedly will. You can also check out *LivingSocial.com* as well for another Groupon style site.

I suspect you are reading this book because you are, or have the potential to be, a cutting edge thinker, and you want to be ahead of the game. You probably already know that mobile marketing needs to be part of your future. It's my hope that *Thumbonomics* helps you move onto that cutting edge sooner than later.

Findability Makeover
Mobile Findability — Your "Other" Computer

The other day my husband and I were disagreeing about super heroes … Yes, we are a geek couple. Specifically, we disputed the name of Aquaman's horse … I reached for my smartphone and had the answer in seconds!

As it turned out, both of our guesses were wrong. The horse's name, in case you were wondering, is *Storm the Sea Horse*.

I started thinking about the nuances of mobile Findability. I wondered:

What is it that makes my smartphone different from my home or office computer?

Efficiency and **immediacy** came to mind right away.

- **Efficiency** because I have my smartphone with me at all times.
- **Immediacy** because I can get an answer FAST, no matter where my job might take me. It doesn't matter whether I'm ten minutes from home or across the country.

How can your business effectively leverage Mobile devices and be findable to prospects this very moment?

The fact is that a smartphone and a home computer have become less and less different over time. Obviously, I wouldn't edit a Word document on my smartphone but I do use it to search for *restaurants, suppliers and retailers* as well as check my email and social media portals.

On the road, *Foursquare.com* and *Yelp.com* are my primary resources to find restaurants, deals, tips and offers that may be in walking distance of my hotel or conference center.

Findability Challenge

How does a business use sites like *Foursquare.com* and *Yelp.com* to *geo-target* prospects, for the highest possible Mobile Media marketing Findability?

Action Plan

- Identify your local Mobile Portals such as *Yelp, Foursquare* and *QR Codes.*
- Use keywords properly in Mobile Portals.
- Encourage conversation and empower your "fans" to promote you.

Step One: Identify Your Local Mobile Portals

1. Setup and claim your *Yelp.com* account.
2. Setup and claim your *Foursquare.com* presence.
3. Create a *QR Code* and actively use it on all marketing material.

Step Two: Use Keywords Properly in Mobile Portals

1. **Use keywords** *in Yelp, Foursquare, Company Name or Nick Name.*

   When you "Unlock" your business in Yelp, *make sure to use the keyword in your company name,* for instance, "Findability Group Search Marketing." (Search Marketing is our key word phrase.)
2. **Use keywords** *in your company descriptions and offers.*

   Use your keyword phrases in your descriptions. Make sure to link to those pages in your site whenever possible.
3. **Create custom landing pages** *for Yelp and Foursquare company URL's.*

   Co-brand your pages with phrases such as: *"Thanks for Visiting us from Yelp!"* Give them a special offer for Yelp visitors only. Create a unique URL such as *http://www.YourDomain.com/YelpOffer*.

Step Three: Encourage Conversation– Empower Fans to Promote for You!

Whenever happy customers compliment your services or products, encourage them to review your business on Yelp. Always have some kind of special offer set up with Four-square, such as a small gift or discount.

Your ad will stand out and be noticed. Chili's offers free chips and salsa when you show your waitress their special offer code in Foursquare.

You will need to actively solicit positive comments from happy customers. Otherwise, frequently the only reviews that show up will be the negative ones. Reviews and comments provide powerful decision-making criteria for prospective buyers.

Even if your business is not a store front, these sites can help your Findability inside of Yelp. Post your Yelp, Foursquare or QR Codes on entry doors, table tents or any marketing materials you mail to clients.

Mobile Marketing has been the buzz for years; only now are we seeing real Findability results with these portals.

As a smart business owner, use these sites for optimum Findability, and don't forget—they work like search engines. You MUST use keywords wherever possible if you want to be found by the people who don't know your company exists. After all, you want everyone to know your company exists, don't you!?

Rule of Thumb

Mobile use will only expand. Each generation of smartphones brings out more features than few could have imagined a few years ago. With your thumbs, you have far more power than the astronauts who ventured to the moon had.

Companies will tap into the mobile power that keeps them connected with their customers and products. Booting up a computer will become *passé*; with a swipe of a finger and a few taps, the world comes to you.

Josh Alves, used with permission

You just finished this chapter. Congratulations! Now tell us what you think, the tools you use and get additional offers and giveaways. Scan this QR Code with your smartphone or go to *Findability.com/Thumbonomics12* for more Mobile insights.

13

Productivity Tools

Tools for the Individual and Small Business Managing a Social Media Program

If by now, you have read all my suggestions for using the five main social media portals, and your head is spinning—it's about to get much easier. You'll be delighted to hear that along with the growth of social media, tools have been developed to make social media marketing for business easy. These tools allow you to monitor exactly what is happening online, help you rapidly build your community, and easily feed that community with highly relevant content.

I've previously mentioned one of our clients, Keegan Gerhard, owner of the Denver restaurant, *D Bar*, and judge of the Food Network Challenge. When we took Keegan on as a client, he was lucky enough to already have a huge fan base. Not only did he have nationwide fans who watched him on television, but also many locals here in Denver who absolutely love his dessert and wine bar.

Although he had a burgeoning fan base, he was neglecting them. Our goal was to allow Keegan to engage with this fan base in a meaningful way—but one that didn't require him to sit hours a day at his computer. After all, he's a busy chef and TV host, not a computer geek.

We made his social media program simple, yet fully authentic—by automating it. I'll bet you are pleased to hear that! We set it up in levels, starting off with the easiest possible tools.

This same ease is available to you, in the form of social media productivity tools. To decide which are right for you, consider who you are and the size of your business.

Level One Productivity Tools

Perfect for a solo-preneur, small business, or someone just starting out in business. The following three tools are appropriate for someone who will most likely have to manage their social media program on their own: *HootSuite.com*, *SocialOomph.com* and *TweetDeck.com*.

1. ***HootSuite.com*** is a dashboard that allows you to manage multiple social networks in one place. It helps individuals and organizations use the social  web to launch marketing campaigns, identify and grow their audience, and distribute targeted messages across multiple channels.

    HootSuite allows you to spread out your social media communication to Twitter, Facebook, Linkedin and various other social networks all from its easy-to-use dashboard, plus track campaign results and industry trends to rapidly adjust tactics.

    When you log onto HootSuite, you can watch everyone who is talking about you on Twitter, Facebook, and other social media portals. You can assign specific projects to different people: for example, your PR firm, marketing agency, or webmaster. HootSuite makes it easy to manage multiple users over various social network accounts.

Here at the Findability Group, we write all of our tweets and wall posts a month in advance. This gives us a coherent program designed for specific goals, as opposed to randomly making them up as we go along.

Then we go into HootSuite and schedule them, perhaps four a day—early morning, mid morning, lunchtime and mid afternoon. We don't do as much on weekends, because we've noticed most of our communication happens during the week. So, with one meeting, we have accomplished all our tweeting and posting for the entire month.

Using HootSuite to automate your posting lets everyone get back to work. As the folks at HootSuite like to say, "Save your time and save your sanity."

This multi-tasking site will also integrate with Google analytics and track clicks for you. HootSuite lets you take a good look at metrics, to see whether your social media efforts are paying off. (More on that in Chapter 14, *Measurements That Matter*.)

A basic account on HootSuite is free and good. My advice: go there and check out what it can do for you! The free account is very good. There is also a Pro version, when you're ready to upgrade to a higher level of management including multiple accounts and different user groups for minimal dollars.

Scan for more information on *HootSuite.com*

2. *SocialOomph.com* is another fantastic free tool for managing a social media program. It's one  of the first tools I came across when I started doing social media many years ago.

What I like about it is the feature that allows you to automatically follow people who follow you if you choose. This saves you a lot of time and your "Friends list" builds itself. On the other hand, some companies choose to follow just a select few. There are pros and cons to auto-following. Pick the strategy that works for you.

Initially, I followed everyone—anyone who followed me, I automatically followed them. When the numbers added to thousands, I found myself paying less attention to my own Twitterfeed. The solution was to strip my feed of anyone that I didn't personally know or their product—I unfollowed them. Now, I trust my Twitterfeed— everyone who is posting is someone that I want to follow … and hear from.

Every time someone new follows you, SocialOomph automatically sends them a nice, customizable thank you note that you've created when you set up your account.

Don't try to sell them anything in the thank you note. Let them know the kind of content you're going to be giving them on an ongoing basis, maybe give them a link to your website, suggest that you have regular postings on the Facebook fan page for following and say thanks— then be done.

There's been a lot of conversation around social media and auto-following. Should you or shouldn't you? In my mind, if you are using social media for marketing your business—you definitely want to auto-follow as many people as possible.

During one of my trainings, a woman raised her hand and asked, *"How can I un-follow the people that I don't want following me?"*

Hmmm … Why would she want to do that?

I replied, *"Well, here's the deal. If these are personal friends and family members, you can certainly do that. But looking at it from a marketing standpoint, you want to have as many people following you as possible. I say to leave them."*

She wasn't satisfied with that answer. *"But what if she's a porn star?"*

The fact is, your aggregate list of friends on a social media site is no reflection of who you are as a business owner. Please don't stand in judgment of the people who want to follow you. Why discourage them? Twitter has its own system of recognizing spam accounts. If it determines that the "follower" is not a true follower, the odds are that the account will be deleted. My advice is not for you to spend time putting energy into tracking down every follower.

When I discovered this woman was a children's book author, I asked, *"Don't porn stars have children?"*

"Well, yes, I suppose they do."

Case closed.

There is no way to know why a porn star was following a children's book author. We can never know her intent. Perhaps she was just a fan. So, my advice is: initially follow everyone who follows you, and thank them all.

SocialOomph also lets you schedule posts and tweets. It has many more unique features, so take a look at this excellent free tool. They also have a Pro version.

GoogleAlerts and SocialOomph have similarities. At the end of the day, each sends a recap of anyone who has used your name in a tweet, @reply, sent a direct message to you or retweeted one of your postings. Make sure to set up the alerts as a digest to be sent to your email at the end of each day.

Scan for more information on *SocialOomph.com*

3. *TweetDeck.com* has functions that are very similar to HootSuite, but they each have a totally different look and feel. I recommend you test them both to see which one you prefer. Which interface do you like best?

TweetDeck call themselves *"your personal browser for staying in touch with what's happening now, connecting you with your contacts across Twitter, Facebook, MySpace, LinkedIn and more."*

With TweetDeck, anyone can tweet like a pro. See what people are saying about you and join the conversation by tweeting, sharing photos, videos or links directly from TweetDeck. This tool is the ideal choice when you have a huge Twitter community, or you anticipate building a huge Twitter community.

One of our clients is WM Barr, a large corporation with many different product lines including Goof Off, Damp Rid and Sprinkle Rite. They need to manage multiple different social media campaigns for the multiple different product lines.

TweetDeck would be an excellent tool for them to easily manage all their Twitter conversations at the same time.

Scan for more information on *TweetDeck.com*

Level Two Productivity Tools

If you are a small business that is already using social media, you might have a team of social media managers. Once you have set up the **Level One Tools** and have begun building a social media community, you'll need to know how to easily and effectively feed this community.

It's time to move on to syndication tools such as Ping.fm, Twitterfeed, and TubeMogul. With these tools, you can place a blog post or tweet in one location, and they blast it out to a bunch of other social media portals.

1. *Ping.fm* is about content syndication. Among other things, it manages Flickr, the photo-sharing site. If you post photos on Flickr, they will automatically be sent to all your other

communities. It also will help you manage Delicious, NING, GoogleBuzz, and *30 other tools.*

Here's how it works: you put a post, a tweet, or a photo in one location, such as Flickr or Facebook, and Ping.fm sends it to all the other social media sites and social media syndication sites—automatically. This really allows you to make the most of your time and effort. Your content is now reaching a much bigger audience.

Not only are you feeding your Twitter followers and Facebook friends, but you're also getting the word out in other kinds of places, sort of like a press release on PR Newswire. You can take one piece of content and syndicate it across a huge group of media outlets.

Once Ping.fm is set up it is completely automated. Consider the tremendous potential here for connecting to a larger audience and new customers.

Scan for more information on *Ping.fm*

2. *TwitterFeed.com* is an RSS content updater. RSS stands for "really simple syndication." People subscribe to blogs

and news feeds via RSS. TwitterFeed sends your blog posts automatically to Facebook, Twitter, etc.

I'm assuming that by Level Two, you've already got a blog with RSS set up on your website. This makes it easy for people to monitor and watch what you're doing every day or every week, because they see it as soon as you publish new content. TwitterFeed picks up this new content and pushes it out to your Twitter followers instantly.

Twitterfeed updates to any platform that has an RSS feed. Use it to leverage and manage RSS feeds, eloquently and simply.

Scan for more information on *TwitterFeed.com*

3. *TubeMogul.com* is all about syndicating video. If you upload a video onto YouTube, you're only inside the YouTube community.  If you upload it to TubeMogul instead, it is distributed to multiple platforms that house video information, like Blip TV, YouTube, Edge Cast, and the other big video distribution websites.

TubeMogul also produces beautiful analytics. It tells you how many times your video has been viewed. It shows you geography of where your unique audience is. You can even find out how long people viewed your videos, and more. TubeMogul gives you some meaty analytics and feedback about your video efforts.

TubeMogul will syndicate one video to many different platforms to really make the most of the energy you put in to producing it. All for free.

Scan for more information on *TubeMogul.com*

Level Three Productivity Tools

Are you a corporation with big social media campaigns to manage, along with search engine marketing teams or social media marketing teams? The purpose of these marketing teams is to manage content, and listen to what's being said about you. It's their job to keep the buzz going.

Charlie Cole, VP of Marketing for Lucky Brand Jeans is a missionary when it comes to tracking. In my interview with him, he said:

Everything we do is tracked beginning to end. If I post something on Facebook, it is going to have tracking with Facebook that will tell me the number of interactions, number of age views, how long did people look at the post and how many fans looked at it—I will know the total engagement on Facebook. If it's a clickable link where they click off the site or if they click into an application within Facebook, it's going to be tagged so that it links to my back-end web analytics.

I can tell you that the most money we made was $700 a month online—now we are making over $9,000 just from Facebook. I know that's a small number for a multi-million dollar company like us. But, if you convey the idea that this can contribute $250,000 on the bottom line by investing more into what we are doing to grow it.

All promotions have to be trackable—both online and offline.

Facebook isn't the only place that Lucky Brand Jeans is visible. Their YouTube videos are highly watched and used to educate the consumer, and yes, pitch their jeans. They use a variety of tools, simple and free as those on Facebook and others that have a fee attached to them.

To assist your marketing teams, there are two more advanced tools I recommend, *Radian6.com* and *Trackur.com*. These tools are pricier, but you'll receive advance tools and reporting that can do much more than HootSuite or Tweet-Deck for your investment.

1. *Radian6.com* is one of the most expensive tools on the market, at the time of this

book publishing. But it gives you the most comprehensive tools. It has all the features of a HootSuite and a TweetDeck. It can syndicate your content across a wide array of social sites, like *Ping.fm*.

What makes Radian6 worth the expense?

It allows you to identify the strong voices in your industry. Who has already gotten the ear of the social community in your particular field? It will find the sites and groups where your customers and potential customers are already hanging out. You can start identifying and really feeding those groups meaningfully because you know where your prospects already are.

Very valuable information!

With Radian6, you can take the feedback you're getting from your social media community and assign it to different departments in your organization. If a tweet comes in about customer service, Radian6 lets you assign that tweet to a specific customer service rep. You can track whether or not the tweet was ever responded to by that customer service rep. You'll be able to thoroughly track and monitor aggressive communications about your products and services, and the company overall.

Radian6 is very advanced tool. It's suited to supporting huge corporate social media objectives. If you want to see more about what they can do for your organization, sign up for a free demo. These webinars are 30 to 45 minute, live web presentations with one of their account managers.

Scan for more information on *Radian6.com*

2. *Trackur.com* has a slightly lower price point. Trackur is software to monitor and track trends in social media, just like SocialOomph and TweetDeck.

They claim to be the easiest and most affordable social media monitoring software for business—even offering a money-back guarantee.

You can use Trackur to follow overall sentiment about your company. If there is an online uproar over your newest product line, or a heated controversy over something your CEO said— you're going to be able to track that with easy-to-read reports. Trackur is great for a smaller social marketing team, or a small-to-medium sized company that can't afford Radian6.

Scan for more information on *Trackur.com*

Keeping Pace with Social Media and its Applications

I have to admit, writing a book about social media is a bit ridiculous, since by the time it's published and you read it, much of the information is likely to be out of date. Feel free to reference *Findability.com/Thumbonomics*, as we'll be constantly updating information about these tools.

To stay on the cutting edge, you'll want to schedule quarterly meetings with your social media marketing team to evaluate the new tools on the market, and new social sites that have taken off.

Be sure you are using the most efficient tools for your social media efforts.

You'll get very comfortable with the tools you are using, but be aware of when it's time to move on. When I first started doing social media management, TweetDeck was my favorite. As my sophistication grew over time, I transition into HootSuite. Now I'm using HootSuite Pro.

Whether you're a solo-preneur, a small business with a little bit of experience in social media, or a major corporation tackling social media head on—we've given you a wide range of tools to choose from.

A Message to CEOs

Don't be a Chief Ignoring Officer ... Be a Chief Listening Officer. Be willing to really listen to what people are saying about your products and services. Be prepared to give meaningful feedback. Be willing to monitor and listen to sentiment about your company.

It won't all be good. You'll have to be willing to accept the good with the bad. It can be very difficult to keep a finger on the pulse of what people are saying about your company—but you must do exactly that.

These productivity tools give you the power and the management skills to do it effectively, whatever level you are at. They give you one centralized resource to manage your outgoing communications, as well as everything people are saying about you.

Use of any of these tools will be a huge time saver and social network builder. This applies whether you have one person handling your social media campaign, or a team of fifty. I know these tools will be extremely valuable to your organization, and make all the difference in the success of your social media campaign.

Rule of Thumb

Without programs like SocialOomph, HootSuite, TubeMogul, Ping.fm, Trackur, Radian6 and TweetDeck, attempting to stay on top of any strategy that includes the Internet would be comparable to herding cats. Work with the ones that your team decides best suits your needs. It will save a significant amount of time, reduce stress and frustration and supply data so that you can monitor what works and what doesn't.

Romancing the Customer

In the summer of 2011, Lucky Brands Jeans launched the Summer of Love campaign. Carried across the social media portals that their customers frequent—Charlie Cole has said:

(continued)

We're telling this romantic story online and on Facebook, giving people a chance to engage and tell us who their favorite "style" icons are, and that sort of thing.

It connects directly to our clothing launch. Facebook in particular, and social media in general, gives us an opportunity to romance the consumer and not hard-sell them. People aren't on Facebook to be sold things, they're on your fan page because they love the brand.

We want to meld these two ideas: we want social media to be a revenue driver and we want it to be profitable, but we also want it to be this bastion of our brand—we want to give the consumers a little more of the back-story, since they had the wherewithal to like us and stick with us.

Charlie Cole, along with the others quoted throughout *Thumbonomics* "get it"—the power of social media has greatly enhanced their businesses. Read the full Lucky Brand Jeans interview and learn how Charlie Cole and his team have enthusiastically integrated social media in Lucky Brands Jeans.

You just finished this chapter. Congratulations! Now tell us what you think, the tools you use, and get additional offers and giveaways. Scan this QR Code with your smartphone or go to *Findability.com/Thumbonomics13* for more Productivity insights. Download the pdf or audio of the full interview with Charlie Cole of Lucky Brand.

14

Measurements that Matter

Determining Whether Your
Social Media Goals Are Being Met

Picture this: It's May of 2009 and I'm speaking to a CEO group at the Vistage International conference in Chicago, Illinois. A man strides up to me after my presentation, in a Stetson hat, starched, pressed Levis and custom-made cowboy boots—and introduces himself.

This gentleman turned out to be Mark Weiler, the president of Parelli Horsemanship. He asked me to come down to Pagosa Springs within the next 48 hours and meet with his boss, Pat Parelli, and their social media and leadership teams.

Pat Parelli, Heather Lutze and Linda Parelli

Have you seen Robert Redford's *The Horse Whisperer*? Well, Pat Parelli is the man that movie was based on. He invented the phrase *natural horsemanship*, just to give you an idea of his status inside the horse community. Of course, Pat is a rancher—a cowboy—not a technology guru. When he whipped out an iPhone, I was quite surprised.

"Pat, what's your favorite app?"

"Little lady, it's the Fart App."

Yes, the Fart App. I suspect that is as progressive as Pat wants to get, from a technology standpoint.

However, their online community was huge. When my team first met Parelli Natural Horsemanship and explored all their platforms, we identified that they had rogue accounts all over the Web. They had a loyal, international following

Thumbonomics

and a huge number of evangelists talking and tweeting about them. But, Parelli themselves had not captured their space. They weren't fully leveraging their huge public notoriety.

Fortunately, their president was savvy enough to realize this online fan base was something they needed to track, connect with and develop. For Parelli, it's all about building customers who buy their products every month and go to all their events—horse people who are very loyal and passionate about what Parelli Natural Horsemanship does and says.

We gave Parelli Natural Horsemanship a *four-step process* to track the return on investment (ROI) from their social media program.

> I've mentioned this before, but it's worth stating again—before implementing a social media program, make sure you have group agreement from your CEO on down, that social media should be an important part of your company moving forward.

Phase One—Identify the Business Matrix and ROI Behind Social Media

Let me walk you through each one of these steps. No matter what size business you have, they will apply to your social media ROI tracking goals.

Step 1: Identifying Goals

You need to know:

- Exactly why is social media marketing important to your business moving forward?
- What do you hope to gain from it?

Findability Group works with companies like Parelli Natural Horsemanship all over the world. We've come up with a general list of social media goals in various areas:

- Branding.
- Sales.
- Conversation.
- Sentiment analysis (What's the buzz factor—are people overall happy or unhappy with our product and service?).
- Reputation management (What are people saying about us? Is that hurting our reputation or bolstering it?).

Most likely, you have other goals that are specific to your organization. It's not an uncommon factor to hear the following, when we first sit down with new clients: *"We've got a specific product launch,"* or, *"We have a marketing campaign we need support with."* You may have other goals as well.

Assistance with branding, sales and conversions are the most common requests that the Findability Group receives. Reputation management and strategies of how to maintain it has also become a huge part of why a company gets involved in social media.

We know that Google and the other search engines are watching all the social media sites. They are indexing Twitter's tweets; public pages on Facebook; and LinkedIn profiles.

My question for you at this point is: When you type your company's name into a search engine, do you own every single listing in the search engine results page under your name? If not, this might be one of your major branding goals.

You will be setting up different social media accounts to fill all those spots. If you have competitors ranking under your name in Google, Yahoo! or Bing, this gives you the opportunity to dominate that page. After all, that particular page in the search results *is your brand*!

When you search "horse training" and "horse training problems" in Google, you'll see Parelli's website. There are also lots of other things you'll see ranked there. You'll see YouTube videos. You'll see tweets. You'll see blog posts. All are essential for reputation management and branding. Remember, our end game for Parelli is "world domination by keyword phrase" by whatever tools are at our disposal. This includes their website, their blogs, their videos and all social media site accounts.

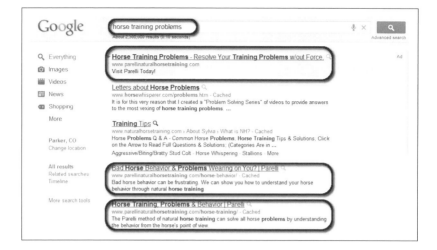

If Parelli Natural Horsemanship could dominate the entire page under the words "horse training," with their YouTube videos, their tweets, or their blog posts—that would be ideal! In the search engine world, domination of the first page is critical—most seeking information stop there.

Step 2: Assigning Measurements to Each Goal

Now we're really getting into the meat of the matter. What measurements or key performance indicators do you need, to know your social media program is working?

What tools do you use to get this information?

If you put people into a social media effort, how can you tell you are getting a decent ROI from those extensive man hours?

That question leads to the specific information you need to know in order to be able to assess the effectiveness of your social media efforts. Let's look at this for each of the goals I just mentioned:

- *Branding*: To measure branding, you're going to be looking at friends, followers, likes, comments and subscribers. You're also going to be looking at the size of your community and your overall share of voice in your industry.

  If your main competitor has 15,000 Twitter followers and you have 5,000 Twitter followers, clearly they have a larger share of voice. It's a concrete measurement, a benchmark you need to meet or beat.

  LinkedIn can tell you how many people have viewed your profile and if your profile is being ranked by Google. Your tweets, YouTube videos and blog posts should also be ranking under specific keyword phrases. These are manual assessments you need to make.

- *Sales*: To measure sales, take a look at Google Analytics. It's free of charge and very easy to configure. Just Google it and you will find tons of tutorials on how to use it. You have no legitimate reason not to incorporate it as part of your routine assessment process!

  Pay close attention to shopping cart interactions. Are you losing people as they move through your shopping cart? Or are they finishing with a purchase? Where did they come from?

You can set up goal tracking for the individual social media sites. You could do specific goal tracking for a product launch. You could do specific goal tracking for a video.

One nice thing about Google Analytics is that it can filter out referrals from specific social media platforms. You can filter out everything else and just see sales that converted out of Facebook. Or out of Twitter. With this information, you'll know that you're really getting a return on your investment for that particular social media sales initiative.

How do you know a sales initiative is working? We call them "yeses" on your website.

- Yes, I would love to watch your video ...
- Yes, sign me up for your newsletter ...
- Yes, I want to subscribe to your blog ...

Videos and newsletters are warming people up before they take the decisive action of buying something from you. From a sales point of view, you want to get lots of yeses, so that you reach the *ultimate yes*—a purchase from your shopping cart.

You may also look at sales from a lead generation standpoint; your main purpose might be getting leads from your website or leads from your blog, an article posted, etc.

Make sure that you're really clear about what outcome you want.

- *Conversation:* To measure conversation, try the tools for tracking conversations recommended in Chapter 13, *Productivity Tools. HootSuite* and *TweetDeck* are ideal and easy to use. Specifically, you need to look at DMs (direct messages) in and also @*replies*.

  They show whether or not you are getting back and forth communication—a key ingredient in a conversation in Twitter. You say something, and someone says something back. And if they like it, perhaps they'll share what you had to say with their community.

How can you track and monitor conversations?

Always look at comments and video responses. If you set up a group in either LinkedIn or Facebook, you can easily see if people are joining the group. Are they re-tweeting or direct messaging you, or emailing you? Any interaction is good interaction, good conversation. Get those conversations going!

Why is conversation so important?

If you're just pushing content out to your social media networks and you're not getting conversation back—you've got a problem. If you're not having two-way conversations, assess the situation. Perhaps you need to stop talking about yourself, stop being so "sale-zy" and really engage in meaningful conversation. What do your readers want to know? What interests them?

Are people recommending you on LinkedIn? My experience with LinkedIn is you have to reach out to people to get recommendations.

Every now and then, I'll have a little gift show up in my LinkedIn recommendations from someone who attended one of my trainings or speeches. When they give me an unsolicited LinkedIn recommendation—that just makes my day.

- *Sentiment*: To measure sentiment, there's a fantastic tool called *TwitterSentiment.com* which will weigh your organization's sentiment overall on Twitter. I also like *SocialMention.com* to monitor what people are saying. Do people really like you, or not?

  If something controversial occurs in your organization, there may be a lot of press or conversation about it. To keep a barometer of when it spikes, you can use *TwitterSentiment.com*. As you talk about what you're doing to address that issue, or clarify what's really going on, your overall sentiment should fall more toward the positive than the negative.

  For a company, it's a good idea to know what the buzz and sentiment factors are. With *TwitterSentiment.com* and *SocialMention.com*, you can track them.

Two other ROI tracking tools which give you an excellent barometer of sentiment are: *Radian6* and *Trackur*. They're both pricier tools, but you pay more for them because they actively manage and monitor sentiment.

Do you have any idea how people feel about your business, overall? You need to start paying attention, not only to the good but the bad. When I talk to business owners, restaurant owners in particular, they're very, very frightened of a negative review.

Review sites and comments are a mixture of negative and positive; it comes with the territory. But, the negative seems to get all the attention. One nasty comment or bad review has everyone running around your office like chickens with their heads cut off.

I find interesting how much feedback and energy we give to negative conversations versus positive conversations. Negative feedback will happen, so have a policy set up-front about how to handle it.

Now, there are situations where mediocre companies found that negative publicity actually brought them more business because of the search engine rankings!

In 2010, an article appeared in *The New York Times* print and online editions about an eye glass company. It had an unbelievable amount of negative postings about their service, the quality, the ineptitude of the staff, of outright lies—the list was huge! Pages of negative postings could be found on *RipoffReport.com*. Yet, when "eye glasses" was searched, it continually came in on the upper page of Google. When customers lodged complaints directly to management, their astonishing response was that they didn't care.

Since *RipoffReport.com* is so actively ranked and monitored by Google, this company believed that a negative sentiment posted there was actually better for them. They got a high quality inbound link to their website from Ripoff Report, which helped their overall ranking! After repeated requests from the public to monitor and fine-tune how rankings are reported, Google has adjusted their algorithm for this sentiment from these negative review sites like Ripoff Report and others.

- *Reputation Management*: Your company's reputation is out there. It matters to stakeholders, employees, customers and the community. The media tracks it and is the first to report on any negatives; often the last to report on any positives.

  How do you stay on top of it? It's one of the most frequently asked questions I get in gatherings of CEO groups. My response is:

  You can have it one of two ways. Either you have someone tap your shoulder at a

Thumbonomics

conference and tell you the awful thing they read about your company—or you can receive an email the minute something negative gets indexed by Google and be the first to know.

If you find out first, you can head straight to your marketing team or PR team, and address the situation in a calm and rational manner. As opposed to being mortified at a conference in front of your peers because they knew before you did.

Google Alerts or a service like *TweetBeep.com* can give you that edge. If someone is upset with you, you'll know as soon as they put it on any social media. This will go a long way to protect your brand overall. Stay ahead of what people are saying—so you are the first to know, not the last.

Step 3: Benchmarking—Know Where You Are Right Now

Where are you at in terms of social media right now? Your benchmark might be that you have no social media yet, period. Perhaps you are just getting your social media accounts set up now. Perhaps you started something a year ago and it's been sitting, stale and inactive. That is the baseline indicator of where you started. You must know exactly where you are, to get to where you want to go.

If you have already started with social media, if you have a blog or a Facebook page, if you are starting to tweet—what tools are you using to handle the whole thing? How have you been tracking your results?

With Parelli Natural Horsemanship, we needed to take a good look at exactly where they were, to determine what they needed to do to meet their goals. Parelli had all these evangelists who were so crazy about the company, that they set up rogue sites and communities of their own. But the company had never set up an official Parelli presence on any of the social media sites. They had no professional accounts that were truly their own.

We changed that by inviting all those rogue evangelists and fan communities into one centralized, official Parelli home. You can view it at *ParelliNaturalHorseTraining.com*.

Step 4: Monthly Metrics Report

Each department, from sales, to customer service, to order fulfillment, to the executive team, needs to know exactly what their social media goals are—and what metrics matter to them.

The sales department might have a specific goal for new leads generated. The order fulfillment department would be looking at the total orders coming in every day—are they increasing? Marketing might be interested in conversions, or video views. They might be watching for an increase in "likes" or "shares."

You need unilateral agreement around what metrics matter each month. Come up with a unified report that becomes a dashboard of dollars in, dollars out. We put this many man-hours in … we're using these specific, finite tools … these are the results we need to see.

You know what your key initiatives are for the coming year. If you are going to support them with social media, you need to start tracking monthly. Decide, as a group, which tools will give you the accurate reporting and metrics you need from month to month.

Phase Two—Keeping Your Social Media Program Alive and Well

Once you have moved through these four steps, gotten all your different social media going, and started using tools for tracking, you will initially see a big growth spurt. You're actively following people that are your clients, people that are your prospects, maybe even going into competitors' sites. You're conversing and connecting with everyone you know.

Eventually though, the growth of the program is going to flat-line, because you've saturated everyone who already knows you. My estimate is you're going to flat line between six months and a year depending on how aggressively you've been building your community.

What do you do now?

1. *Check your tools.* Make sure the webmaster hasn't deleted your icons from your website or disconnected your Google Analytics tracking by mistake, while doing some other work on your site.

There are lots of different reasons why Google Analytics might stop working. Before you jump to any conclusions, make sure that you check all those variables of what might have turned that data off.

2. *Brainstorm ideas with your team for reviving the flat-line.* How about a Twitter contest? Or a creative video that all your employees can participate in? (See the Findability Workshop photos taken onsite at Parelli headquarters on the next page.)

3. *Look at what your competitors are doing in their social marketing, or follow all their friends.* People who search a competitor's topics would probably be interested in your topics as well. That's one way to go after new followers.

4. *Check your followers.* If you're carefully crafting tweets, painstakingly coming up with rich, interesting content, wouldn't it be nice to know if you're getting followers from them or losing followers? To find out, try a great new website called *TweetEffect.com*, which is still in beta at the time of the publication of this book. This tool will tell you which specific tweets are working for you, and which tweets are not, if you've lost followers or gained followers as a result of any tweet. Keep experimenting, adjusting, and tracking what works and what doesn't.

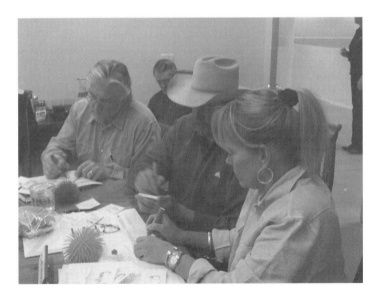

Findability Workshop on site at Parelli Headquarters.

Findability Makeover
In Focus: Parelli Natural Horsemanship

Building and solidifying the relationships that matter most to your company—your customers—is what this Findability Makeover is all about.

Reinventing Relationships with Your Customers Online

Companies spend millions each year asking agencies and marketers to brand their companies in order to reach more prospects. But, how often do these same companies look carefully at the brand that is already built for them by their loyal, current customers? Like it or not, your "fan base" already has built your brand. They hold your company's reputation in the collective palms of their hands, through an aggregate of blog posts, review sites, videos, and social media platforms stating everything they love and hate about your brand.

In the event that this is prominently positive, how do you get these people to collectively support your brand as a community of evangelists for your company? The answer is to start loving your devotees, and to give them what they want—a place to network, talk, share advice and continue to preach about your brand.

In the end, this is what large corporations pay the big bucks for—reverse marketing by and for your already loyal customers, and the best part is it's something you can do yourself.

Introducing the Official Parelli

In May 2009, Parelli Natural Horsemanship found themselves in a predicament. Company founders Pat and Linda Parelli had built a tremendous brand and huge following of horse owners and horse enthusiasts. However, the brand was fragmented and un-controlled online.

For years, Parelli had been known for their passion and love of horses, but they had struggled to produce a website that would support their loyal fans as well as perpetuate a brand that would speak to new prospective customers.

Their Findability problems resulted from an incomplete vision of their online audience and potential reach. Their website did not provide enough of a forum for their fans to express their devotion (*UltimateParelli.com*). As such, YouTube videos, blogs, un-official Facebook fan pages, etc., were appearing across the web.

In many cases, they were pulling away from the core values and mission of Parelli. Additionally, unless a prospect knew to search for "Natural Horsemanship" (an expression the company coined), or for "Parelli," they would not find any official Parelli Natural Horsemanship pages in search results. A searcher looking for "horse training" (167,000 searches per month) would be ideal for Parelli—they were utterly un-findable to this larger audience.

The Problem

How do you "feed" a community of loyal customers to continue to build your brand from the inside out, as well as open the market and build brand awareness to valuable, new prospects?

Findability Score

Back in May 2009, we checked their ranking in *WebSite Grader.com*, which ranked the site at 63 percent and in *SEOMoz.org*, which scored a mere 8 percent. After running the site through our Findability scoring system, we give their site a 43 percent for overall Findability. They were very visible under "Natural Horsemanship" but nowhere to be found under "horse problems" or "horse training," as well as non-existent in the Social Media that thousands of their loyal customers were communicating in daily.

Action Plan: Reinvent *Parelli.com* Brand Inside and Out!

Parelli Natural Horsemanship needed to go big or go home! In an effort to establish their online brand, they went all out and decided to redesign their website, rewrite all the content for SEO (search engine optimization) and start aggressively utilizing social media to congregate their followers! This was a big job with a big potential payoff.

The Solution?

Tip #1: Love Your Domain Name & Show the Search Engines You Care: Select a Domain Name For Findability—It Matters!

Their old domain was *Parelli.com*. There were some inherent problems with this domain name. Yes, it is the name of the founders Pat and Linda Parelli but there is also a Tire Company with a very similar name, Pirelli Tires. (A very easy mistake to make if you do not know how to spell Parelli correctly.) They also wanted exposure under the keyword "Horse Training." One of the keys to success was to change the primary domain to *ParelliNaturalHorse Training.com*.

Parelli is now ranked multiple times under Horse Training and under Natural Horse Training, and has increased their exposure by more than 167,000 searches per month. Now that's building a brand—and true Findability.

Tip # 2: Build New Website Look and Feel Consistent with Mission

Their old site lacked focus with too much going on, including over 60 immediate "options" for what the user could do—essentially, the clear action for a user to take was "do everything … now." Also, the home page was used as a clearing house for products on sale, giving them the image of being the Wal-Mart of horse training. People who came to the home page needing help with their horse were being sold horse accessories.

The end result: very confusing messaging overall and *not* consistent with their message of "Love, Language and Leadership" with your horse.

On the following pages you will see the before and after—the "before" reflects their original site; and the "after" emulates the elegance of the Parelli Natural Horsemanship method and exhibits great Findability.

The new website makeover included:

1. Clearing out the clutter and cutting to the chase.
2. Four primary conversion opportunities are presented on *every* page of the website.
3. The leather background is now consistent with their other product lines designs.
4. Pat and Linda Parelli are front and center on the home page and every interior page.

5. Finally, Pat Parelli recorded a custom "welcome" video on the home page just to add a more personal touch. Now they present a cohesive user experience that appeals to both the long time devotee of Parelli, as well as the first time visitor looking for guidance with their horse.

Tip #3: Setup Social Media for Huge Community of Followers Waiting for Your Lead

Parelli had not established a social media presence. A large community of devoted followers were building their own rogue Facebook pages and waiting for Parelli to establish their official Facebook presence. We recommended setting up "official" Parelli Facebook, Twitter and YouTube accounts to hold their name as well as establish a credible place on these social media sites that their followers could trust.

Their followers wanted access to Pat and Linda Parelli, and now they have it. Parelli has created a strong social media presence and their followers have responded in droves with 53,000 Fans on their Facebook Fan Page, the 22nd most popular new YouTube Channel and over 5,700 followers on Twitter.

Parelli has succeeded in manifesting a huge number of customers and devoted fans who evangelize their brand for them every day.

Taking the plunge and reinventing yourself or your business is scary, but even scarier is the inability to adapt and change over time. The Internet is a very fast paced environment and you must stay in touch to discover any mistakes you may have made in your branding, and be willing to make it right. Ultimately, Parelli is seeing big payoffs and great Findability for being bold and taking a stand for who they are as a company. Bravo Parelli!

Search

Parelli Natural Horsemanship
Education · Pagosa Springs, Colorado

Wall   Parelli Natural Horsemanship · Top posts

Share: 🖼 Post   Photo   Link   Video

Write something...

 Parelli Natural Horsemanship added 21 new photos to the album Fast Track, August 2011.

Fast Track, August 2011
A few informal photos from the Fast Track course taking place right now at the P...
See more

 5 hours ago · Like · Comment · Share

 54 people like this.

 Uta Peters Universe: let me win the lottery so I can go one more time ! My 2 weeks 'Liberty and Horse Behaviour' a few years ago in Ocala was Hands down THE BEST vacation I ever took. Those pictures bring back wonderful memories!
5 hours ago · Like · 👍 2 people

 Janicia West Ditto on the lottery thing!
4 hours ago · Like · 👍 1 person

Write a comment...

 Parelli Natural Horsemanship
We've just added a great new feature to ParelliConnect.com to help you on your journey: E-Learning will help guide you toward new heights in your horsemanship! Level 1 is now available, and the rest of the Levels are on their way. If you're not a member yet, sign up for a free 30-day trial and try it out! http://ow.ly/67Vfs

Linda Parelli tells you about E-Learning in Parelli Connect [HQ]
Length: 1:38

Left sidebar

We Are Parelli WORLDWIDE

Help Us Grow by 10,000 Members and
TOGETHER WE WILL GIVE AWAY $1 MILLION ▸
in educational material to four main equine causes.
32%

You Spread the Word. We Donate.
Horses and Humans Win

- 📋 **Wall**
- 📄 Info
- ◈ Fan Offers
- 🏆 Contests
- ◈ $1 Million Giveaway
- 📅 Events
- ◈ Sponsors
- ◈ Facebook PicBadges
- MORE ▾

About

Welcome to the Official Parelli Natural Horsemanship fan page! Check back...
More

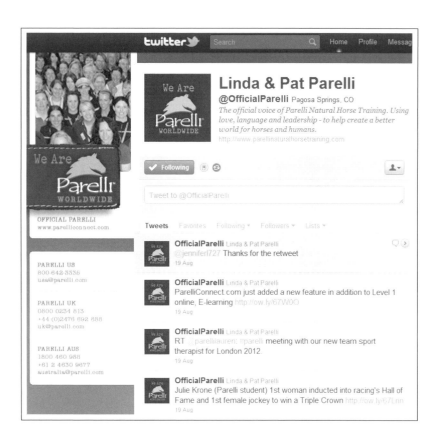

Thumbonomics

Rule of Thumb

When you sit down in a year from now and look at what you've done, here's what becomes evident:

- You will see exactly which goals you did or didn't meet.
- You'll see exact measurements of your social media program's success.
- You will have a clear picture of what you accomplished—what didn't quite work as expected, and where there is more work to be done.

Using Google Analytics to tell you if you're really getting people to convert is a critical element to your mix. Are visitors having conversations with you? Are they

(continued)

filling out contact forms on your website? And the bottom line—are they taking that final action—purchasing?

That's the information you need to show everyone in your organization that social media is a viable marketing tool; one that's fully measurable; and one that provides a big, exciting, meaningful ROI.

You just finished this chapter. Congratulations! Now tell us what you think, the tools you use, and get additional offers and giveaways. Scan this QR Code with your smartphone or go to *Findability.com/Thumbonomics14* for more Measurements That Matter insights.

15

Your Social Media Program– Outsource or In-House?

See What's Out There—
What Can Serve You Best—and Decide

When it comes to deciding whether to do your social media marketing in-house, or outsourcing it; there are various considerations. Consider doing what you do best, and outsourcing the rest. After all, no one can talk about what you do day-to-day better than you and your staff.

Colorado's Governor John Hickenlooper strongly believes in having youth on his team. He strongly believes that it's important to pay attention to kids. When asked what advice he would give to business owners and looking for innovative ways to market, he answered:

I don't know anything except what I've learned from my nephew and niece and some of my younger staff members. It's important for people, old fogies like myself, to stay connected and aware of what the new, cutting edge media are. Familiarize yourself with what's out there.

Don't try and be something you are not. Don't try and pretend your business is going to do things it doesn't. Social media can expose fraudulent claims and insincere positions.

What Kind of Things Should You Outsource?

During the initial setup of your social media accounts, there are various best practices and findability options you need to execute. But, you might not have the time, the manpower, or the expertise. Here's where to start:

1. **Custom backgrounds**: Hire professional designers for certain elements of your profile setup. Use a custom background for Twitter, not the standard backgrounds they offer.

    Go to a tool like 99 Designs or *elance.com* and look for someone who's willing to do a custom background for your Twitter or Facebook account. (That should only cost about $100.)

    Take a look at my Facebook profile (*Facebook.com/FindabilityGroup*). You'll see I have a custom banner running down the side. It has a unique selling proposition, my contact information and icons for my other social media portals—all in all, it looks extremely professional.

2. **Naming conventions of your accounts**: Do they have your key words in them? Is that something you need help with, if you don't know much about SEO or keywords?

3. **Privacy settings appropriate to your objectives**: Do you know, or have someone on your team who knows, how to set them up correctly?

4. **Professional photos:** If you have a nice headshot, use that. Don't use a photo that you took at the company Christmas party or one someone snapped of you just sitting at your cubicle.

    For the Findability Group, I made sure all the women had their hair and makeup done. We all wore similar colors, with nice backgrounds. The photos were professionally shot because in all our social media portals, it was important to me that my staff feel good about their photos and their voice. If you are asking anyone in your organization to be publicly involved in social media, make sure they have professional photos they are proud of.

5. **Setup of productivity tools**: These are the ones we referred to in Chapter 13, *Productivity Tools*. If you don't have time to manage these tools, consider outsourcing the management and uploading of your content into a tool like HootSuite or TweetDeck.

Handling Your Social Media In-House

If you prefer, your entire social media campaign can be done in-house. If you want to handle it that way, here's what I recommend:

1. **Hire a dedicated intern or assign an entry-level person to specifically handle your social media**

campaign. When Colorado's Governor John Hickenlooper kicked-off his campaign, he strongly believed in having youth and interns on his team.

Place an ad in Craig's List, or tweet it. Get someone fresh-out-of-college, preferably with a marketing degree; start him or her off with a low wage. It should be easy to find a college grad for this position—and he'll probably think it's the coolest job in the world. After all, most of the college crowd are doing social media for themselves anyway, and are quite proficient with it.

Check out *Findability.com* for complete social media manager and intern job descriptions. You can post and tweet these job descriptions, to make sure you are hiring someone with the right skill set for these particular positions.

Have your intern read *Thumbonomics* so that he gets the big picture, and understands exactly what protocol you want followed.

An intern coming in at $10 an hour might or might not be able to build a custom background for a site, but could certainly handle the outsourcing of that kind of work. He or she will undoubtedly be delighted to get this kind of on-the-job-training.

2. **Have a specific plan of action.** Meet with your intern and social media team. Each department contributing anything to social media should give their report…"Here are all the things that we're

going to do this month ... Here are the video assets we have this month ... Here are the blogs ... Here's the newsletter content ..."

Gather all this data and hand it off to your intern. He will then parse it out into tweets, wall posts, blogs and video posts for your YouTube channel. Your intern's job is to make sure that everyone knows about all the content, all the doings, all the press releases, all the product launches—whatever's happening inside your organization.

Use your intern to make sure you're really accessing all the right resources, and getting out all the content that you really want your followers to see.

3. **Set up Plug-Ins or Connection Applications which allow you to propagate your content dynamically to Twitter, Facebook, LinkedIn and YouTube.** In this way, every time you put a video on YouTube, it is automatically shared to your Facebook and Twitter communities. You can stream your tweets right on your website's home page; into your LinkedIn page; and right onto your Facebook wall automatically.

Make sure that whoever is managing your social media effort is dynamically propagating all your content from one centralized source, by using one or more of the productivity tools we mentioned in Chapter 13, *Productivity Tools.*

For instance, *Ping.fm* will syndicate all of your social media from one centralized portal.

4. **Become savvy in using Productivity Tools to reduce negative effects.** If there is ever any negative reaction to something you posted, using these tools will allow you to push it down faster and more efficiently. They simply make centralization of content distribution much easier, especially if you're doing it in-house.

Training and Conferences for Your Social Media Team

I cannot recommend this highly enough if you really want to be a success in social media marketing. I send my employees to at least two conferences a year. I believe it is absolutely essential that they hob-nob with specialists in their fields, and get to know the people who are doing the same kind of work.

Essential Conferences I Recommend

I urge you to consider these particular search marketing conferences. There are many other conferences happening. But, I trust these three explicitly—they are the ones I send my own employees to. You'll not only be able to mix and mingle with people who are doing social media and SEO as a profession, you'll also meet a lot of other business owners.

1. **Web 2.0 Summit** is the main one I recommend (which takes place annually in San Francisco in the

fall). Web 2.0 is where leaders of the Internet economy gather to debate and determine business strategy. Attend Web 2.0 to really move onto the cutting edge of what's happening in social media marketing. Their site: *Web2Summit.com.*

2. **Search Engine Strategies** has conferences all over the country. They have conferences specifically for mobile marketing, social media marketing and other specialized topics. The biggest events each year are in New York City, San Francisco or San Jose. Their site: *SearchEngineStrategies.com.*

3. **Online Marketing Summit** enables attendees to collaborate, network and learn how to execute the best practices in online marketing *with no exhibit floor or vendor sales pitch distractions.* If you go to their site, you'll see all the different marketing summits they have all across the country. I spoke at a couple of their events last year and hope to do so again this year. I found the quality of their presenters to be excellent. Their site: *OnlineMarketingSummit.com.*

4. **PubCon** is my final recommendation. As we all know, most of the good networking at conferences happens in the hotel bar or in the hallway. Now, don't get me wrong. You don't go to a conference to drink—but usually you do end up doing that anyway. PubCon gives attendees a great opportunity to network with new friends and business contacts in relaxed, informal

surroundings set in a Las Vegas pub-like environment.

PubCon is about all things web-related. Make sure whoever is managing your social media gets a wide variety of education, not only to social media but website and search marketing strategies, blogging, and video preparation as well. PubCon always has some of the most exciting, informative speakers around, on a wide variety of topics. Their site: *PubCon.com.*

When deciding which conferences to attend, it's important not just to go to those devoted to social media, but to all kinds of Internet oriented conferences that give you a wide breadth of exposure to different topics.

When you do attend a conference, bring a huge stack of business cards. There is a lot of cross-over in this industry, which is important because you need to meet a lot of different people. Give out and collect as many business cards as you can.

You literally cannot make too many contacts.

As soon as you or your social media manager returns from a conference, look up all these new contacts on LinkedIn right away. Send each person a personal message: *"Great to meet you; can't wait to connect and link up."*

In this way, you build an arsenal of resources for your social media manager or intern. It's invaluable to have access to knowledgeable people you can reach out to, or ask questions of. Particularly people you have actually met, face-to-face, at a conference or training.

These new contacts will also build your LinkedIn community. Invite them to collectively start sharing questions and resources as a group. That's an incredibly powerful resource to have as you grow your social media program.

Essential Trainings

Findability (SEO) Training

- **Michael Marshall** (*SearchEngineAcademy.com*): I highly recommend Michael Marshall, of the Search Engine Academy. Michael is an innovative software developer, trainer and consultant in the search industry and does trainings all over the country. He will come in-house and train your staff on search. Or consider attending one of their bigger, group events, run by Robin Nobles and John Alexander.
- *BruceClay.com*: It offers the SEOToolSet® Training. This is a multi-day training on search engine marketing that is incredibly helpful.
- **BlogWorld & New Media Expo, Las Vegas, NV** (*BlogWorldExpo.com*): The Blogworld and New Media Expo combines a traditional conference with a grand social media exhibition where attendees can view and interact with the latest in every sector of social media, from mobile technology to the

newest social networking tools. The conference portion of the weekend covers strategies, techniques, and tools that have helped the most successful social media giants achieve their goals.

- **Digiday: SOCIAL, New York, NY** *(DigidaySocial.com)*: Digiday: SOCIAL brings together some of the top leaders of the social media industry in order to provide attendees with unique insights into social media strategy issues, and how the future looks for the field. Past speakers at the conference include representatives from BlogHer, Toyota and more.

- **Schmoozd, Santa Monica, CA** *(Schmoozd.com)*: Schmoozd is a unique conference experience that does away with traditional presentations and panels in favor of an open format where social media professionals can meet other professionals, share strategies and contribute to the exchange of ideas. Attendees choose categories and topics that they are interested in, and meet people who are interested in the same issues.

- **Social Media Strategies Summit, Boston** *(SocialMediaStrategiesSummit.com)*: The Social Media Strategies Summit is for executives and managers of social media companies and any business that could benefit from the exciting field of social media marketing. Conference topics will include both the basics and more advanced issues, such as microblogging and maintaining online communities.

Those are the trainings I feel are absolutely essential, but of course, there are many more available. Don't forget to visit *Findability.com*. We keep abreast of all the newest strategies and trends in internet marketing. An active list is kept of all the resources and websites we believe will be the most valuable for you.

Rule of Thumb

The question for you to ask now: Is it time to switch from in-house to outsource?

It's important to know when you've reached your threshold, when enough is enough and you just can't manage it in-house anymore. Be willing to pull resources in—whether an agency, specific designers or content writers. Don't hesitate to outsource whatever you cannot manage in-house.

Using a carefully considered mix of in-house and outsourced professionals gives you the best shot to handle social media correctly and effectively. It allows everyone to do exactly what they do best, and helps you provide high-quality content over time—content that people will truly want to follow.

You just finished this chapter. Congratulations! Now tell us what you think, the tools you use, and get additional offers and giveaways. Scan this QR Code with your smartphone or go to *Findability.com/Thumbonomics15* for more insights.

16

Upcoming Trends

Even More Big Changes Are Coming in Marketing Due to Social Media

I'm often asked these questions: What's next? What's the next big thing? What should I be looking out for as I build my marketing strategy for the coming years?

I believe the biggest trend in the next few years will be *social media websites.* In other words, websites that are not the same, flat or static. Similar to WordPress blogs now, websites will all have interactive components; components that let you share every single element of that site. Every website will have an RSS feed, so followers can stay up to date with any changes to the content.

With a social media website, each page on your site would allow comments. Customers can post their interactions with your company, experiences they had, results they gained. You'll see social media icons on everything. This is already becoming prevalent, and I think by the end of 2011, we will see them everywhere.

I believe we will see more innovative ideas in website design, and rethinking of standard formats. Does a site have to have a Flash component? Or can it just be a WordPress site, which is completely content based?

In Boulder, Colorado, there is a multi-million dollar company called *Sparkfun.com.* They sell all sorts of gadgets, gizmos and electronic tidbits to the hobbyist and electronic enthusiast crowd. SparkFun Electronics' website, albeit very simple, is loaded with tons of content in a WordPress style format. For more amazing, big brand WordPress sites go to *wpbeginner.com/showcase/21-popular-brands-that-are-using-wordpress/*.

Scan this QR Code to visit the blog "21 Popular Brands that Are Using Wordpress" posts.

Most websites have been the same style for years. The top navigation always has "about us," "services," "testimonials" and "contact us." This kind of site will start looking very old and very passé—very "old school." You're going to see a new style emerge that is based more on first person engagement.

Following the lead of social media, there will be a multitude of different ways people can interact with your website, not just via the "contact us" form.

You and I will be able to:

- Engage on their Facebook page …
- Follow their tweets …
- Subscribe to their blog via RSS feed …
- Receive their newsletter …
- Watch videos on their website …
- Comment on every page …
- "Like" a button on every page and blog post.

The engagement level will go through the roof!

As a forward thinking CMO or CEO of a company, you'll recognize the need to have all different types of engagement opportunities, not just good web content. In fact, these days, content is probably the last thing anyone wants to look at on a website. People want to be informed while being entertained. What's the fun factor of your site?

Apps and Innovations

I think we'll see the "apps" trend continue to move forward. Huge numbers of apps already exist, and many more will be built—apps for everything you can think of.

After years of only being a PC owner, I recently purchased my first Mac product—the iPad, and I created *Thumbonomics* on a MacBook Air. I have to tell you, I was a little reluctant about moving into Mac technology. It's always annoyed me that there seem to be two separate camps: Mac enthusiasts versus the PC crowd. Why can't we all just get along? Are they really that different?

Since using my iPad, I've realized there is a highly intuitive nature about an Apple product. The way the screens open is entertaining. Even the way you touch the screen on an iPad is very engaging. It's innovative.

I love the iPad not because it is an Apple product, but because it's sexy, it's clean, it's elegant looking, and it's light. These are things people are inherently attracted to. It just so happens that Apple—the company building these products—and they have made them super-sexy.

Because of this, I've come to love my iPad much more than my PC.

I strongly believe that the engagement level is the main component people are responding to with Apple products. Engagement that is intuitive is what's important right now. It is the engagement level that will mean the most to your business in terms of online marketing.

I now see PCs as extremely utilitarian and work-related. In contrast, I see my iPad as a source of entertainment and fun. Even though I do work on my iPad all the time, I am able to engage with it at a whole different level.

Not to belabor the point—but companies have practiced for years what Apple does so well. Women purchase Coach and Louie Vuitton handbags to be considered sophisticated. Ditto for the Starbucks latte or simply holding the cup with the Starbucks logo on it. Today, having an iPad or iPhone is considered trendy.

Mobile Marketing—The Time Has Come

Mobile marketing is another trend that will be interesting to watch. I remember being at search engine marketing conferences five years ago, and hearing about mobile marketing. Everyone wanted to get excited about it, but no one was really going for it as part of a small or medium sized business marketing initiative. The majority of companies had many other marketing priorities.

But now, most companies have followed through with their website initiatives, and are launching into social media initiatives. I believe mobile marketing's time has finally come. With the introduction of QR codes, mass marketing is at your customers' fingertips.

Although mobile technology is growing very fast, I find corporations in general to be much slower in adopting new technologies. Even one short year ago, I was still occasionally meeting business owners who had no website at all.

What has changed it? The recession in 2009 and 2010 shook people silly. For many businesses it's been a huge wake-up call; one that has shaken them out of their traditional marketing comfort zones of print media, radio, yellow pages, etc.

You know the mentality I'm talking about, the one that says,

Oh, we do that every year, we'll continue to do that.
That'll never change.

This is the first year I've seen companies get rid of their comfortable marketing mechanisms and allocate entire marketing budgets to online marketing, specifically search marketing. And now they are moving on to social media marketing.

I'm so glad to be finally seeing this transformation! The recession has forced companies to look at more progressive and cutting-edge marketing techniques.

Mobile marketing will slowly-but-surely be adopted by companies as well, whether that happens in 2012 or beyond, time will tell.

I predict this to be the year of social media marketing and mobile marketing! Adapt or Die.

Owners, presidents and CEOs are getting their heads around it. They're embracing it. They're dropping their fear and reaching out to connect with customers in meaningful and productive ways they never believed possible.

How about you?

You just finished this chapter. Congratulations! Now tell us what you think, the tools you use, and get additional offers and giveaways. Scan this QR Code with your smartphone or go to *Findability.com/Thumbonomics16* for more trends and upcoming technology insights.

Acknowledgments

There are so many people to thank in the creation of this book, here are the people who without their help, this book would never have been possible.

To Leslie Miller for her amazing editing and writing skills.

To Ronnie Moore of WESType Publishing Services, Inc., her layout work is brilliant!

To Josh Alves for your creative "thumb people" and how they made me smile throughout this book process. *JoshAlves.com*

For Judith Briles and John Maling and their amazing Book Shepherding skills. *BookShepherd.com*

For Governor John Hickenlooper, for giving a budding author time in his busy political schedule to share his thoughts on Social Media and his campaign.

For Keegan Gerhard of D Bar Desserts for making "life changing" chocolate cake and his amazing, heartfelt interview.

For Charlie Cole of Lucky Brand and his insightful, date driven Social Media program.

For Bill Gerth and his Comcast Team. Great interview!

Tony Hseih, CEO of Zappos.com for your vision are a truly innovative thought leader and CEO.

About the Author
Heather Lutze

After 10 years of working with business owners and executives, I have made it my personal mission to stop the "smoke and mirrors" that is Search Engine Marketing. I feel strongly that business owners, marketing executives and web site managers can manage their own web site's "Findability" and save thousands in the process.

After years of being a graphic artist and owning my own website design business, I decided it was time to stop building "un-findable" websites. So I worked for a dot com and had the opportunity to work with millions of dollars in ad revenues within a very young internet marketing world. I worked with the major search engines and learned the huge issues about websites and the ways in which searcher's need to find your site.

At one fateful search marketing conference, I met one of the founding members of the original Yahoo! team and we hit it off. I then went to work for Yahoo! Search Marketing for three years, training advertisers how to spend their money to get more business. During this time, I learned what the Findability Formula was all about. It was never about the website, it was about how the searcher needed to have the website be present when the need presented itself.

I am now a nationally recognized internet marketing speaker, trainer, and consultant in search engine marketing including SEO, Paid Search, and Social Media Marketing Findability. My speaking engagements are conducted in the same easy, understandable style as my bestselling book *The Findability Formula: The Easy, Non-Technical Approach to Search Engine Marketing* published by Wiley & Sons—delivering equal parts good information and good entertainment to audiences nationwide.

I am proud to be a member of the National Speaker's Association (NSA), the Colorado chapter of the NSA, and the Meeting Industry Council (MIC). I re-certify every year in Google AdWords and have trained for PPC (Pay Per Click) Summit for three years. For the last two years, I have been a monthly columnist for Website Magazine doing Findability Makeovers for website business owners.

In July of 2000, I founded the Findability Group in response to all the web site owners who had paid for web sites that weren't performing. It was my clients' frustration with getting traffic to their sites that was my inspiration for learning and mastering the art and science of search engine visibility. We now have fifteen employees and growing. We specialize in customized Search Marketing Solutions in Pay Per Click, SEO, and Social Media Marketing for "World Domination By Keyword Phrase!"

What Findability Group Does Best!

The Findability Group Search Marketing Company is a full service agency specializing in Search Engine Optimization, Paid Search (PPC) and Social Media Marketing for Findability. Below is complete list of our offerings.

Full Service Agency

Custom search marketing campaigns, which include a combination of PPC, SEO, Social Media and website project management. This is the best, brightest group of people I have ever found. They love what they do and it shows!

Findability Consulting

Professional Guidance in one-on-one consultation on Search Engine Marketing.

Executive Coaching Program

Website and Search Marketing analysis and monthly coaching with CEO Heather Lutze on aligning your team with a successful Search Marketing Strategy!

WE HAVE FUN! No ... really!

Findability Training and Workshops

Custom training programs (either half day or full day) to educate your team on the basics of Search Engine Marketing, Paid Search and Social Media best practices for Findability.

Full day workshop with you and your team, includes a custom training on the three pillars of Findability (SEO, PPC and Social Media) and a custom-built Search Marketing strategy for your business.

Findability Speakers

Heather Lutze and the Findability Team travel the world speaking on Findability for such prestigious corporations as IBM, Calamos Investments, Tony Robbins Business Mastery, Parelli Natural Horsemanship and events such as Online Marketing Summit, PGA and many more.

Findability University

Your online source for the most up-to-the-minute tools, information and resources to enhance your online marketing efforts.

For greater detail about The Findability Group Search Marketing Company and its services visit our website or call our offices.

www.Findability.com
303-841-3111

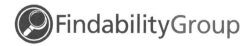